MW00809528

PRAISE FOR *SEEING THE HOW*

"Today's most successful new innovators don't look to just reimagine products; they look to reimagine consumer experiences—the way we do the stuff of daily life. This is the powerful idea driving Allen Adamson's new book, *Seeing the How*, which he supports with a combination of compelling storytelling and prescriptive guidance. Both a fun and practical read, marketers in every category will enjoy and learn from this engaging book."

—Suzy Deering, former Global CMO, Ford Motor Corporation

"Allen Adamson's new book, *Seeing the How*, is a valuable guide on how to see—and seize—the next innovative opportunity by identifying ways to make the things people do every day even better."

—Bob Pittman, Chairman and CEO of iHeartMedia

"Don't ask 'What?' Ask 'How?' In his new book, Allen Adamson makes clear that competitive marketplace advantage is now achieved by savvy businesses transforming not just products but the experiences of life, making them more desirable and better in some never imagined way. *Seeing the How* is both a fun read and instructive."

—Antonio Belloni, Group Managing Director, LVMH

"Allen Adamson is one of the most experienced and insightful marketing observers; he brings unique perspectives to the most difficult and perplexing marketing problems. With an impressive track record of industry leadership and business best sellers, Allen's latest, *Seeing the How*, astutely shifts the innovation focus for marketers to customer experiences. Skillfully blending classic ideas with fresh thinking, Allen once again breaks new ground on a critically important marketing topic."

—Kevin Lane Keller, E. B. Osborn Professor of Marketing,
Tuck School of Business at Dartmouth

"Don't assume people won't change the way they've always done things. Offer them a better, more compelling option, and they most certainly will. That is the powerful idea behind Allen Adamson's new book, *Seeing the How*, which makes evident why success now belongs to companies transforming the experiences of daily life. It's both persuasive and practical."

—Tony Leopold, Senior Vice President of Strategy,
Digital & Business Development, United Rentals

"Successful innovators don't look to reimagine products; they look to reimagine consumers' experiences—the way we do the stuff of daily life. Allen Adamson's *Seeing the How* is both entertaining and enlightening. It's a must read for anyone looking for the next breakthrough opportunity."

—Gary Briggs, former CMO, Facebook

"I've long said that what the business world today most needs is experience innovation. *Seeing the How* makes the case for this, and (not surprisingly) shows you how."

—B. Joseph Pine II, Coauthor, *The Experience Economy: Competing for Customer Time, Attention, and Money*

"In *Seeing the How*, Allen Adamson shares the secrets and insights of those disrupting the market, not by focusing on changing products but by changing how consumers do things. Offering a wealth of examples, he persuasively argues that it's not by asking 'what' but 'how,' that today's savviest marketers are finding dramatic ways to grow brands."

—Noah Brodsky, Chief Commercial Officer, Lindblad Expeditions

"We hear a lot these days about creating brand differentiation and customer value through 'the customer experience,' but it's hard to really find good examples and concrete specifics. In *Seeing the How*, Allen Adamson provides these necessary case histories and ground-level details about how these market-winning experience innovations were conceived, as disruptive out-of-the box ideas, and then executed. A fun and practical read, this book will motivate and enable you to create the types of customer experience innovations that will help your business win in today's experience-driven marketplace."

—Rajeev Batra, SS Kresge Professor of Marketing, Ross School of Business, University of Michigan

"Why is it that in so many companies the desk farthest from the front door is where the person in charge sits. Allen is talking about getting to the front lines."

—Paco Underhill, Author, *Why We Buy: The Science of Shopping*

"In *Seeing the How*, Allen Adamson reinforces the important role consumer experience plays in building successful brands. At Sony, we strive to fill the world with emotion, through the power of creativity and technology. We learned early on the power of being able to transform how people consume entertainment. The Walkman revolutionized how people listen to music, changing listening habits forever. It wasn't the technology, per se, it was changing the consumer experience that upended the industry."

—Steven Fuld, Senior Vice President, Marketing, Sony Corporation

"Any marketer—wait, any businessperson, from aspiring entrepreneur to Fortune 500 CEO—worth their weight has a working knowledge of human-centered design and the principles and practices associated with customer centricity. The genius of Allen in *Seeing the How* is that he reveals how you're supposed to use such an approach to not just 'paint by numbers' but instead create something with a distinct point of view that sets you apart. Through dozens of examples, he shares why the new generation of businesses, which are rapidly becoming the stuff of boardroom and classroom legend, are those built on reimagining how people do everyday things . . . and importantly, how you can, too."

—Dr. Samantha Sterling, Chief Strategy Officer, AKQA

SEEING THE HOW

ALSO BY ALLEN P. ADAMSON

Shift Ahead: How the Best Companies Stay Relevant in a Fast-Changing World

The Edge: 50 Tips from Brands that Lead

BrandDigital: Simple Ways Top Brands Succeed in the Digital World

BrandSimple: How the Best Brands Keep it Simple and Succeed

SEEING THE HOW

Transforming <u>What People Do</u>, Not Buy, to Gain Market Advantage

ALLEN P. ADAMSON

Matt Holt Books
An Imprint of BenBella Books, Inc.
Dallas, TX

This book is designed to provide accurate and authoritative information about marketing. Neither the author nor the publisher is engaged in rendering legal, accounting, or other professional services by publishing this book. If any such assistance is required, the services of a qualified financial professional should be sought. The author and publisher will not be responsible for any liability, loss, or risk incurred as a result of the use and application of any information contained in this book.

Seeing the How copyright © 2023 by Allen P. Adamson

All rights reserved. No part of this book may be used or reproduced in any manner whatsoever without written permission of the publisher, except in the case of brief quotations embodied in critical articles or reviews.

Matt Holt is an imprint of BenBella Books, Inc.
10440 N. Central Expressway
Suite 800
Dallas, TX 75231
benbellabooks.com
Send feedback to feedback@benbellabooks.com

BenBella and *Matt Holt* are federally registered trademarks.

Printed in the United States of America
10 9 8 7 6 5 4 3 2 1

Library of Congress Control Number: 2022045489
ISBN 9781637742952 (hardcover)
ISBN 9781637742969 (electronic)

Editing by Katie Dickman
Copyediting by Lydia Choi
Proofreading by James Fraleigh and Cape Cod Compositors, Inc.
Text design and composition by Aaron Edmiston
Cover design by Chuck Routheir
Printed by Lake Book Manufacturing

Special discounts for bulk sales are available.
Please contact bulkorders@benbellabooks.com.

For Joe E. Adamson

This book is essentially about the lenses through which we view the world—the lenses that determine how and why we see what we see, which, in turn, shape our beliefs, our thoughts, and our actions. There have been several lenses through which I have viewed the world over the course of my life, be it from a parental perspective, a career perspective, and even as a citizen of the world. More than any other, the lens that has helped me see more clearly how to live a positive, productive, and appreciative life is the one through my father's eyes.

With great love and gratitude, I dedicate this book to my father, Joe Adamson, who passed away in 2022 at the age of ninety-seven after an early life overcoming extraordinary challenges, quietly and humbly cherishing all that came after.

He was not your "average Joe."

(Please see the acknowledgments in the back of this book to read more about the extraordinary challenges Joe Adamson overcame early in life.)

Contents

Introduction

One of my favorite parts of my life is heading down to Washing-
ton Square toward the NYU Stern School of Business. Once there, I take
the elevator up to the fourth floor, where the Berkley Center for Entrepreneurship is based. For many years now, I've been fortunate enough to be the
center's branding person in residence. This means that I meet on a regular
basis with groups of student entrepreneurs from different schools within
the NYU ecosystem, including the business school, the engineering school,
and the Steinhardt School of Culture, Education, and Human Development.

In any given session, I listen to their ideas. Thrown open to the best
form of groupthink, these ideas are sharpened, interrogated, and strength-
ened, and their narratives expounded upon. We talk about how to bring
those ideas to life, how to brand them, how to communicate what is different about them, and why people should care. Hearing those fresh ideas
emerge from an individual or a group and then working with them to learn
how to think, discern, and create is one of life's great pleasures.

Four or five years ago, more than a few students of mine encouraged
me to listen to an NPR podcast called *How I Built This*. It wasn't just one

or two of my students telling me; it was a *lot* of them prodding me to take a listen. When I next had some downtime, I explored the show and its library of episodes. It didn't take long before I was hooked. It was winter break, and it quickly became my routine to start my day with a walk on the beach, headphones on, listening to Guy Raz tell the story of how brands with companies and products that are now everywhere started their journeys, as well as the challenges they faced. Listening to it was a true pleasure.

MARKETING IS WHERE IDEAS ARE BORN . . .

After many pleasurable hours listening to the podcast, it struck me how so many of these new businesses over the last five to ten years found their success not by inventing something new nor by developing some new technology. They hadn't contrived to bring to this world the newest and best mousetrap. These companies had instead looked at what was going on in the marketplace and had seen an opportunity to take what I call an "off-the-shelf" idea or technology and reconfigure it in a way that would change how people do things.

Having grown up in the world where we marketers market the next new thing—with the emphasis on "thing"—this was a rather revolutionary idea. No more waiting for someone to invent, test, and release something that I, the marketing person, would then shovel out into the world. Marketing people, I realized, really shouldn't be waiting for someone to give them something new to market. The marketing people are the ones in a position to be the idea originators, the concept builders, the ones who put the "start" in "startup." Marketing people understand the marketplace, they understand consumers, and they know what those consumers like and don't like about the way things are going at any given time. At least, the good marketing people do. And thus, the idea for this book first germinated.

I know I leave my students with a lot to think about—in terms of what has worked and not worked in the past but also about how to be their own best think tank, how to parse and unpack their ideas so they can understand why they may or may not work, and how best to go about putting them into action. But I've learned so much from my students as well. I was left with this kernel of an idea about the new stage of innovation being about someone looking at what has always been done in a certain way and offering a new way to do it, a new experience of what has always been with us. I'm equally grateful for the work Guy Raz does to tell the stories of the companies that shape all of our daily lives and to do so in a compelling and inspiring way for so many.

The idea of innovation being about a change of behavior and not about a shiny new object stayed with me as I guest-lectured in Professor Eitan Mueller's entrepreneur class a few weeks after my deep dive into Raz's podcast. After class, Eitan and I caught up over coffee in the courtyard in front of the business school.

As we sat there, Eitan mentioned an idea he'd recently had that he wanted to bounce off me. In a nutshell: while Uber and Airbnb were both extremely successful new companies, he thought only Uber was disruptive in the classic sense in which Clayton Christensen, the Harvard professor who wrote *The Innovator's Dilemma*, describes disruption because Uber had almost vaporized the existing businesses in its space, such as taxis and car services. According to Christensen, disruption is best described as new players that deliver products at a fraction of the cost of current options yet still meet the most important consumer needs. The result, he explains, is that customers will leave the old way and move to the new. Existing leaders flail. New leaders prevail. Disruption occurs. This, Eitan said, was in contrast with Airbnb, which, while successful, had not decimated the other players in its categories. Hotels and other hospitality options were still very much intact and would remain so, no matter how big Airbnb might become. One did not replace the other.

We kicked this idea around a bit. And I acknowledged his idea as an interesting one that offered a perspective from which one could learn and analyze. But our conversation reminded me of what I had thought about while walking on the beach with Guy Raz in my ear. I pointed out that this idea was limited in its use to we who are trying to find a way to think differently and make our mark. I was led back to the idea that in both cases—Uber and Airbnb—the value and the success were found not in making something new, not in creating new tech to do something, but in changing the experience of doing what we were going to do anyway. And that had some traction to it.

Eitan and I agreed that both ideas were interesting enough to be worth considering in a book that incorporated disruption and experience, but, after a couple of months, Eitan's priorities wouldn't allow him the time to tackle a book in addition to everything else. From there, I took the baton that was the idea of looking at how experience innovation was impacting marketing and decided to run with it.

This book is my exploration of the growing group of innovators—smart marketers all—who have transformed the way we live our lives through experience innovation, not product innovation. They've launched companies that have become critical players in a fundamental transformation of day-to-day life—from which you, my dear reader, can learn from and perform your own experience innovations.

WHO THIS BOOK IS FOR AND WHY

When you walk into a marketing class, the whiteboard isn't filled with equations, and there's a good reason for that. For the most part, marketing problems are not solved by putting all the market information into an algorithm, then taking the results and executing them. Marketing is typically about connecting the analytical world to the constantly changing world we live in. This is rarely accomplished by simply adding up a column of numbers.

In my phenomenally enjoyable career in the marketing world, ranging from brand management to advertising to branding to general marketing consulting, what I've loved most about it is the extent to which I have been challenged to bring nonlinear thinking to a rational, linear world. Marketing challenges don't have cut-and-dried answers that allow you to take processes and execute them without nuance. Understanding what data means and how it impacts human behavior, then adding a dash of creativity to that understanding to arrive at an idea or concept that speaks to something others have not yet noticed—this is the art that is marketing.

And the art of marketing is now in a position to address itself to a whole new world, one where marketers drive the changes and transformations of tomorrow. Back in the days of yore (not that long ago), it was marketing's job to understand to whom we should target our pitch, to know which segment of the market was ripe for whatever new thing we had to sell. Because, of course, while everyone wants to sell everything to everybody, success and marketing is about focusing and finding the most likely consumers for this better mousetrap, this product innovation, or that service innovation. But once you identify that core-focus target audience, if you set about understanding how that audience feels and thinks about certain products or services of the kind you want to offer, you can introduce the new in a way that has the best shot of becoming people's new preference—of becoming the new way they brush their teeth, wash their hair, diaper their babies, or clean their clothes.

Claudia Kotchka, my former P&G client who was the vice president of design innovation and strategy at the time, and I talked about how marketers spent so many years marching to a beat established by a band of chemical engineers and PhDs at P&G's research and development. They thought in the narrow space of creating something out of nothing or tweaking the something we already had so it could be sold as something new and improved. No one, as Kotchka put it, "was really thinking about the holistic customer. And I think that still happens today. This is why the lessons we learned from IDEO were so valuable. They came to teach us the tools, techniques, and how to look at consumers differently."[1]

Because P&G's marketing team was intimate with and so often the source of input for consumer wishes—people wanted things to work better, act faster, last longer, clean better—it would identify these points and then pass them along to someone who would try to invent something entirely new that would do what was needed. That person would then pass the baton over to the chemical engineers, PhDs, and R&D folks to develop a better mousetrap, figure out the formulation, and develop a product that would solve what consumers were looking for.

IDEO is a global design and consulting firm that uses a design-thinking approach to create products, services, environments, and digital experiences. While the company started with a focus on designing consumer products (e.g., toothbrushes, personal assistants, computers), by 2001, IDEO began to widen its focus to include consumer experiences and services. IDEO is probably best known for working with Apple to design its original mouse. It also became an important partner with P&G, where Kotchka brought the company on to use its design thinking as a way to look at consumers through a different lens than that of the chemical engineers and R&D people (the departments where traditional innovation had always lived).

While this kind of active search for a new angle on a situation might be the norm in Silicon Valley, what Kotchka did and describes is still quite new to mainstream corporate America. And Kotchka reminded me of the still-true words of Peter Drucker: "It's not about selling. That's not what it is. It's about finding out, it's building a deep relationship with your customer, knowing what it is they want, need, and then [figuring] out how to give it to them. That to me is what marketing is, which is why marketing needs to take the reins in creating the business, not just selling what others make."

This book is about the lenses that marketers wear to see what they see, and how they achieve success by seizing what they see. This book explores why—and how—this new breed of marketers is able to see and seize opportunities to transform human experience and how they go on to achieve remarkable success in their ventures when they set aside visions of creating a new toy and focus instead on how to make life as we live it better. By exploring those who have traveled this experience–innovation path, readers can learn from them, use what they learn to spark their own ideas, and apply the lessons to their own initiatives.

This book reinforces the importance of being able to see things differently in order to be a part of the cultural conversation that consumers are having with the companies that provide their services and goods. These new lenses will allow you to see how today's smartest marketers are finding promising opportunities. This book offers lessons learned from those who know where and how to look, and it makes clear how to use this new spectrum of lenses to your, and your customers', advantage.

SEE THE HOW:
GET READY FOR
EXPERIENCE INNOVATION

We live in a time where it is *experiences* and not *things* that drive us and motivate us to buy, participate, and talk about something. How we experience things dictates where we will spend our money. Yes, you can step into the streets of NYC to hail a cab, but there may or may not be one out there. Or, for the same price (or, sometimes, a lot more), you can order an Uber and know when it will arrive, that it will arrive, and how much it will cost you to get where you are going. That's choosing experience over price in a nutshell.

Organizations are acknowledging this fact in how they do business and what titles they assign to those doing the work. General Mills—a consumer-product behemoth if ever there was one—has shifted the marketing nomenclature from "brand manager" to "experience manager." The distinction is one that is far more important than what is listed on someone's business card or LinkedIn profile; it's about a shift in thinking and role.

CUSTOMERS ARE OPEN TO—AND READY FOR— NEW AND BETTER EXPERIENCES

Experience dominates our timelines, stories, and feeds on social-media platforms, and, as we will see throughout this book, it is increasingly where money is spent and value is placed. Why use a taxi when you can meet someone interesting while sharing a ride through Via? Why fight the corporate battles when you can be part of the gig economy and work from anywhere in the world? Why stay in a nondescript hotel room when you can enjoy a more authentic neighborhood experience in someone's charming London flat? Extraordinary experiences, more so than products, are rocket fuel for word of mouth—no one shares what's average.

From the way we listen to music to the way we bank, shop, invest, exercise, travel, work, decorate our homes, and dine out or eat in, consumers are increasingly open to—and ready to adopt—new experiences. This means that everything about the way we examine and come to understand the economic climate needs to be readjusted. For example, economists have typically lumped experiences in with services, but it's clear that experiences are a distinct economic offering as different from services as services are from goods.

It's important to make sure the distinction is made between what Joseph Pine and James Gilmore coined so powerfully as the "experience economy" and what I'm calling "experience innovation." The former, as Pine and Gilmore so aptly described it, is about taking what people want to buy—for example, Nike sneakers—and recognizing that the sway it holds over people is such that you can add on a layer of experience to that purchase and charge them for it. So the experience economy charges consumers for the experience of buying what they were going to buy regardless.

Experience innovation is different. It's what Pine described when he talked to me about Maxwell House (one of the leading coffee brands of its day) and its failure to think beyond the cup of joe for which it was famous. After hearing one of its senior executives say that there was not much room for innovation in the coffee business, Pine pitched the idea that creating cafés owned and defined by Maxwell House would capture the market by offering the opportunity to sell more than just the coffee through defining the experience that was drinking coffee. Today, this is something we take for granted as we head to Starbucks, which has made itself into something between an addiction-facilitation center and a town hall. Starbucks sells the experience of drinking coffee and all that goes with it. Maxwell House couldn't think beyond the coffee it produced.

Experience innovation is about taking what we already do—ride, invest, travel—and transforming it to be about *how* you go about doing it. In this book, I'll share the secrets and insights of those who are disrupting the market—not through product-based innovation but with innovations that prompt a shift in consumer behavior. We are seeing this group continue to increase in size, playing a fundamental role in economic and consumer transformation.

We know experience innovation is our present and the future. We ride in Ubers and stay with our families in Airbnb residences. We buy our pets their food and supplies online through Chewy, spend evenings binge-watching Netflix, pass afternoons with Spotify playing background music, turn to Warby Parker when in need of new eyeglasses, and subscribe to Dollar Shave Club so that we never run out of razor blades. Our friends show us cars purchased from and delivered to their driveway by Carvana. When we return from business trips, we use Expensify to scan receipts, track expenses, and then sync information with QuickBooks for more efficient review by our accountants. We set up meetings with Calendly and hold those meetings on Zoom. Our kids buy clothing via Stitch Fix and, when they're busy studying, get their food from DoorDash.

As diverse a group as these and many other companies are, they have one thing in common: they have disrupted the status quo by identifying and reimagining a whole new way to provide an overall better customer experience. And they've done so not according to the universally acknowledged benchmarks of customer care. Being responsive to customer needs and delivering a high level of service have become absolute table stakes in today's see-all, share-all environment. Rather, experience disruptors look where no one else has thought to look to shake things up and find a relevantly different way of making the stuff of daily life different and better and easier. They are not doing this by putting new products on our shelves or devices in our hands or technology in our software. They are doing this by rethinking the "how," not the "what." In doing so, unlike traditional product or service businesses that can be readily imitated, they set themselves up for sustainable growth.

When I started at Unilever in marketing, my title was Product Manager. My product: Caress soap. I was product oriented because that's what my company made, and I was there to create interest in and need for that product. In the next chapter of my career, I was on the "agency side" of the business, supporting my client who was the brand manager on Dawn dishwashing detergent. Already a category leader, its success was all about "taking the grease out of your way" for cleaner dishes.

Product and service are tangible things; brand is abstract. Brand is about perception, expectations, memories, stories, and relationships that, taken together, account for a consumer's decision to reach for your product versus someone else's. P&G was masterful at building and marketing brands, and Dawn was its best-case example. P&G could identify a consumer insight related to a problem and articulate how its brand could make life better or easier in some way. While Dawn's initial success was due to a product claim, its subsequent success was due to marketing claims that went beyond the product performance: "Dawn takes grease out of your way to get you out of the kitchen faster because [we know] you've got better things to do." Consumers emotionally connected with this. The promise of a relevantly different product experience proved incredibly successful for the brand. Dawn's branding captured the benefits of an experience.

When I spoke with Douglas Martin, chief brand and disruptive-growth officer at General Mills, he reflected on his sixteen years at the company. As he put it, back in the day, it wasn't about what a customer did with a product or how they experienced it; the big questions were about the products themselves. "'How do we make this bar crunchier?' Or, 'How do we make this thing lower-calorie because that seems to be the direction the category is going?' Now the starting point is 'How do we make people's lives better?' This is an enormously important shift because it truly outweighs and defines anything else you might do or say about a brand."[1]

So marketing job titles shift to reflect what leads to leadership in the marketplace: customer experience, the ways in which what you do makes their lives better. The task may be similar—it still rests on the ability to identify a consumer problem and solve it in a way that is relevantly different. But now, the focus on interaction, which is much harder for competitors to replicate, makes dominance easier to maintain. These new category innovators know that experience is king.

WHAT IS THE CUSTOMER EXPERIENCE?

Your goal is to understand what's working, what's not working, and why. In other words, it is only when you get your head fully in the game—granular, nuanced, and in tune—that you can fully grasp the customer journey in all senses. You need to really understand the customer journey—how customers first heard about your company, your product, or your service and how they learn about it, purchase it, and decide where to purchase it again. You must walk a mile in their shoes.

I'm a visual person, so I prefer to map things out. As I think through what the current consumer experience is today, I think in terms of concrete questions to which I have or can get, more or less, some kind of an answer. My approach is granular by necessity. These questions include:

- How did they hear about the brand? How did they learn about it?
- How did they first see the product? Hold it? Try it? Smell it?
- How did they purchase it?
- What was their experience like upon purchase? Did they carry or drive it home themselves, or was it delivered? Was the process easy? Fast? Consistent from purchase to purchase?
- How was their experience of using the product for the first time? Did they need to read instructions before using it? (This is my least favorite thing to do, which is why I was an early Apple adopter.) Were the instructions long or short, and were they easy or difficult to understand? Were they clearly translated from another language? Was there a YouTube video explaining the product's use? Was there someone customers could call for help if they screwed up? Did the helpline only work Monday to Friday from nine to five, and were customers likely to be setting the product up on a Saturday morning?

Once I have the answers to these types of questions, I pull back a little and examine the industry I am exploring. I look for indicators that it is ripe for a new flavor, voice, or approach. While experience innovation is possible in industries that meet all the criteria for being solidly served by existing companies, it's a good idea not to overlook the more fundamental business dynamics of why companies begin to and ultimately fail. From Kodak to Blackberry to Blockbuster, examples abound. Look for these telltale signs of opportunity:

- Quality improvements stagnate
- Prices increase without a corresponding increase in quality
- Quality improvements are marginal to core value
- There are extremes of revenue deviation—up or down—within a category
- A company is complacent, albeit nicely profitable, but fails to see the writing on the wall

Looking for these signs of opportunity can be as sophisticated as you want to make it, but it must always start with a hands-in-the-dirt understanding of the customer experience. Once you map the journey and identify the touchpoints, you can then use them to figure out what consumers are feeling and thinking. Say you want to know about car rentals from start to finish, reservation to return—how does the process go? Where are the hiccups, the "I wish it could be different" moments? You look at what options are on offer, the pricing, the range of ways the service might be used, and map it all out. This is foundational thinking that must precede all innovation.

An interesting fact about all of this: as you map the customer experience and compare the various ways you and others offer a similar thing or service, you'll find that there is rarely a great difference among the current choices. This is why one of the most important questions to ask is: How are you screwing up? Where, how, and why do the problems occur? Don't focus on the majority of times things go smoothly; drill down on those instances when it all falls apart.

Experience Has Come to Town

It is generally accepted that millennials, as well as every other generation, are opting out of accumulating stuff and are seeking experiences instead.

Lifestyle analyses show mounting evidence that spending on "non-essential" categories, including travel and dining out, will continue to gain over product categories. People want to spend their money on experiences that enhance their lives, speaking to the idea of the "experiential consumer."

These experiences are also what people use to define themselves across social channels, more so than the traditional "badge" brands. Scroll through your Instagram and Facebook feeds, and you're more likely to see a friend's photos of Machu Picchu, their dinner from a food truck in Austin, or pictures of their kids on a beach in Cape Cod than you are to see them bragging about their Prada bag or Rolex watch. It's notable that this is as much about the quest for unique experiences as it is the desire and ability to share these experiences with others. I think we can all agree that it's very easy and far more enjoyable to share pictures from your dumpling-making class than it is to selfie your way through your latest romp through the supermarket.

Customer Experience Is Driving More Growth Than Product Differentiation

There is a new consumer. The "share-everything consumer" wants everyone to see the cool things they are doing. This is nothing short of a seismic shift from the emphasis on getting people to buy your product to one that is all about what they do with it once the purchase is made. If you look at everyday purchases like mobile games, media streamers, and virtual assistants, these are things people still buy. The initial purchase of these things are, in fact, necessary; without them, subsequent activities that make use of them are not possible. But the fortunes of those products are not dependent on the things, per se. Their success comes in how well those things create an experience consumers can have and share about.

While the share-everything consumer may have begun as one of a millennial or youth movement, it has quickly overtaken generations far older. This broad shift in consumer behavior means that these new consumers expect exceptional experiences from businesses and use this metric when it comes down to making purchasing decisions. When push comes to shove, they increasingly place greater value on experiential solutions over product solutions.

This all emerges from the social media–fueled word-of-mouth world in which we all live and that drives the power experience has over product differentiation as a factor in who achieves market success and who does not. The delightful experience gets the shares; workaday and mediocre encounters do not. That which is shared gains a momentum that makes the expression "going viral" send shivers down the spines of marketing executives everywhere.

As Kevin Keller, E. B. Osborn Professor of Marketing at the Tuck School of Business at Dartmouth College, explains:

> Traditionally, the people responsible for positioning brands have concentrated on points of difference—the benefits that set each brand apart from the competition. Maytag is distinguished by dependability, Tide by whitening power, BMW by superior handling. Such points of differentiation are, in many cases, what consumers remember about a brand. But points of differentiation alone are not enough to sustain a brand against competitors. Managers often pay too little attention to two other aspects of competitive positioning: understanding the frame of reference within which their brands work and addressing the features that brands have in common with competitors. There are always circumstances in

which it's necessary to "break even" with competing brands. Effective brand positioning requires not only careful consideration of a brand's points of difference, but also of what we call its points of parity with other products.[2]

These customer points of parity, when undelivered, are anchors holding you back. Points of difference are how you set yourself apart. Both are key parts of the customer journey, and they are pulled together by finding out what people talk about. Customers talk about how things went wrong and ways in which their expectations were exceeded. With that information, you can neutralize your weak links and strengthen the ways in which you differentiate yourself. This is not a revolutionary idea, but understanding what those touchpoints are for you is a vital first step. But it is only the first step.

The conclusion? The difference between one brand and another is shrinking all the time. What matters: experience.

MOVE OUT FROM BEHIND YOUR DESK: MYOPIA IS NOT AN OPTION

Myopia is nearsightedness. Marketing myopia is a focus on what is immediately in front of your nose, the obvious, and it is not an option if you aim to be remarkable. And you need to aim at something remarkable if you want to succeed. Zeroing in on specific benefits or features of a product or service without zooming out and taking a broader look at marketplace conditions, societal trends, and, critically, the evolution of consumer needs and demands is a recipe for being left behind. While this has always been true, the complexity of the market today makes this an even greater challenge.

Perhaps no one understood this more—or better—than Theodore Levitt. A former professor at the Harvard Business School, the 1960 publication of his article "Marketing Myopia" in the *Harvard Business Review* was a defining moment for marketing. Levitt theorized that myopic business decisions are those that feel enough satisfaction with the status quo, believe the positive numbers and growth are baked into whatever they are doing, and stop looking for new ways to serve the needs of their customers. In order for companies to ensure continued growth, Levitt continued, they must define the industry they are in broadly, and, more prescient, he urged companies to define themselves from the perspective of the consumer. People are rarely looking to buy a specific product, he wrote, but a solution to a specific problem.

Some say Levitt's ideas marked the start of the modern marketing movement.

A more current and analogy-focused note on the subject of marketing myopia comes from my colleague and the coauthor of our book *Shift Ahead*, marketing professor Joel Steckel, who framed it this way: to be successful, marketers should be playing golf, not tennis.

To put it simply, in singles tennis, you are one of two players, and you are entirely focused on what the other player is doing—thinking about what they might do next, how you'll respond, and setting yourself up for the shot you think you'll need to take or the one you want to force the other player to make. It's a narrow field of focus, like Coke versus Pepsi or Colgate versus Crest. These are small worlds defined by tiny increments of movement on both sides.

In golf, you are playing against several others. And, yes, you will note how they are playing and the strategy they bring to the game. But your real attention is on yourself first: the quality, strength, and swing that you bring to the ball. Your strategy is there, but you are also noting the course, both what you know of it in general and how it looks on that day in particular. All of the quirks your awareness brings to light will improve your ability to play better than the others. You note the weather, the wind, and how your play will be affected by all of the above, as well as how the course itself will respond to the elements.

In other words, in tennis, you are playing a two-person game in which your battle is circumscribed and your ability to affect the outcome is narrow. Golf, however, demands that you think broadly, widely, deeply, and from a number of different perspectives. There are still winners and losers, and very much so, but what lands some in one category and others in another will depend on their ability to take in the micro, the macro, the personal, the environmental—their ability to speak to and understand the larger experience.

A lack of ability to see a bigger picture, an inability to see the broader societal context, and a lack of intellectual knowledge or curiosity won't position you for a successful venture. The following chapter will help open your eyes (pun intended) to what's required as a first step. But even with curiosity on full display, getting out from behind your desk is a harder ask than you'd think. Look at your day. Do you see a lot of downtime in your daily schedule? How often does your calendar say: "11 AM: go outside, look around, find out where people are going and what they're doing once they get there"?

It's not surprising that when I talked with Faith Popcorn, futurist to the Fortune 500 and someone I've had the privilege of knowing for many years, her thinking was already quite evolved on the topic. In the world of long-guessing what tomorrow will bring, she is one of the best. She has been right a shocking number of times. That what she predicts will come true is a good bet; when that will be, however, can be more difficult to predict.

She talked to me about how difficult it is to get executives, the decision makers, to step out from behind their desks, as well as how vital it is to their business to find that time in their schedule and see that it's just as, if not more, important as the weekly marketing meeting and the R&D pitch.

She is not unsympathetic. These executives are, by definition, a breed that must expend much of their mental energy living in the moment. But they, too, must grapple with the future: How are we going to make this quarter? Do we pay attention to long-term trends? The organization that supports its executives and creates a culture that values making the time and space for decision makers to look up and out will see the benefits.

Listen to the Experiences Your Products Produce

Claudia Kotchka played a key role in figuring out what parents (mostly mothers) want from their children's diapers. She was in charge of P&G's design, tasked with bringing new innovation tools and techniques into the company. But it was incredibly difficult to get marketing on board because the experiences reported by her consumers didn't match up with what marketing thought were the important parts of selling diapers. It was only when IDEO came on and talked about the importance of hearing from every corner of the process and every angle of the experience to be had from your product that they were able to make progress.

IDEO teaches a user-centered, customer-centered design, which means finding out what your customer really wants and then, of course, giving it to them. But discovering the comprehensive sense of what customers want is difficult. Kotchka described how it went when they tried to tackle the Diaper Dilemma. Pampers asked consumers one question: What do you want from your diapers? Answer: no leaks. They thought it was that simple. One question, one answer. Then Huggies came out with a diaper that did not leak but managed to do so with a plastic sheet layer that was soft and quiet. Turns out, *that* was really and equally important. Moms don't want their kids to crinkle when they pick them up, and they don't want to feel like they are wrapping their kids in plastic. This was a much harder answer to elicit organically. And it goes on from there. "No one ever asked for an iPhone, right? They can't tell you; you've got to figure it out yourself," said Kotchka. "I'm still shocked at the number of people today who do focus groups, who go out and ask the customer what they want. It's just a complete waste of time. And so we had to teach people to do ethnography to find different ways to figure out what people need and want and what they do."[3]

Ask the Right Questions

Asking the right questions, then, involves more than just, well, asking questions. Making sure the questions come from different areas and approaches is key.

Many years ago, I worked with Pizza Hut on its branding. Business was pretty good, and we were doing research on how to further strengthen the brand. We spoke with consumers in markets all across the country. We asked questions that probably won't surprise you: How do you like Pizza Hut? Are you satisfied with the taste? The responses were equally banal: Yes, we enjoy Pizza Hut. It's a nice place to eat and it tastes good. It's usually hot; we go there often. And so on.

But there was one moderator who was particularly skilled at asking questions—the right questions. She didn't ask people to tell her about their experiences by saying whether they were happy or unhappy because, it turns out, people don't actually like being negative. They'll say "fine" before they say "bad." Instead, this moderator asked, "If Pizza Hut were to go out of business, what would you do?"

It was a huge "aha" moment—because every respondent, without hesitation, said, "I'd go to Papa John's" or another well-known pizza alternative. No one expressed sadness about the absence of the Pizza Hut option. So, despite having expressed satisfaction with Pizza Hut, it was clear the feeling was devoid of a deep connection.

This brings me to Leslie Zane, founder and CEO of Triggers® Brand Consulting and a leading expert in unpacking human instinct, who started with the simple statement that "companies with high satisfaction rates can still be in decline."[4] In other words, people can be satisfied without forming any attachment to a company or brand. Brand and product strength is not about whether or not a customer is content to go to you; it's about whether or not you and your brand are an entrenched part of their lives.

The other thing Zane explained to me about not asking the right questions is that people will tell you what they think you want to hear, or they'll say what is most immediately on the top of their head, which isn't necessarily their true sense of things. Between this and the fact that habits are hard to break, it's no wonder that focus groups and other attempts to dive deeply into the thinking of customers can be so frustrating.

At the heart of your inquiry must be: How do people live their lives? What do they already use and how and why do they use it? How do they come to decide to make the choices that they do? What are the barriers they experience to gaining access to what they need and/or want? What kind of learning curve can they tolerate, and what is the best means of access to its adoption? When so much comes down to customer service, it becomes one of those touchpoints that, when broken, are so hard to recover from. How are those failures defined?

Broadening our perspective to include the entirety of the customer journey is key, but it isn't a smooth path. As Rajeev Batra, marketing professor at the University of Michigan, puts it so well,

> You need to examine pain points that hadn't been salient before, that create new opportunities to alter how products are built. The whole research approach of looking at the entire customer journey, mapping it, and so on is something that's relatively new to research professionals, and the methodologies are not that common and easy. It's easier to sort of wave your hands and come up

with a customer-journey map out of thin air. How do you actually get the data to have an empirically based, factually based customer journey, such that it identifies the pain points in each stage? This is still challenging in terms of the research methodology.[5]

More Than What Is, Ask How It Might Be

I return to Zane, who explained that the way you understand what customers are really thinking is by giving them permission to free themselves from their fixed view of the world—from this, you'll get at the customer insight that will truly change behavior. "We don't ask people, 'What do you want?' We ask people to create a new thing. We tell them to create their fantasy experience. We invite them to suspend reality. 'Don't worry about how this would be done, or whether it can be done—don't even go there. Dream about how you would want it to be.' And what they invariably do is reach really high."[6] That is the input you want to hear. Those are the answers to "What do you want?" that will drive you toward offering an experience that will transform how someone does something.

Zane offered a great example of this from her experience querying people on behalf of a pharmaceutical company. When asked what their fantasy was regarding their medication, Zane reported to me,

They answered, "I walk outside, and the rain starts falling. And inside the raindrops is this healing balm that comes over me, and my disease is done." Well, what does that tell you? It tells you a lot of things. It tells you that they don't want the medication to be strong; it tells you that gentleness is more important than efficacy. It tells you there's an anti-drug movement, and people don't want chemicals in their bodies. So the idea is really to use the unconscious mind to access the highest-order ideas, which otherwise would be left on the table.[7]

Most of the work Jeremy Dawkins, global head of design at ?What If! (a part of Accenture), does focuses on the challenges that many of the company's clients are grappling with in ever-changing markets. How do they activate an innovative mindset to identify and create opportunities for lasting growth and speak to what does not yet exist?

We talked about the need to start with the human experience, looking at consumer problems from their point of view. Whatever it is that you are going to invent has to fit into someone's life. You can't just have people in a lab exclaiming about what they've discovered yet having no clear idea about what to do with it. Dawkins shared a humorous anecdote about a client in Asia who said they had lots of ideas for 5G technology but that no one was interested—they'd started their efforts without researching potential uses for 5G. Of all the topics we touched on, however, the most important to his work—and to this book—was the necessity of being able to look at the world with fresh eyes and knowing how to hear what is being said to you.

As Dawkins described to me, if you ask a teenage boy how long he spends at the mirror grooming his hair—once you've defined what "grooming" means—his answer will be a fraction of what actually takes place in his room or bathroom every morning.[8] No one likes to self-report the effort and time they spent that others might consider a waste. Yet we rely on understanding what is happening in the minds, homes, offices, and cars (among the many spaces we inhabit) of our fellow humans in order to do the work of improving experiences.

It's time to get your head in the game and get inside the head of your customers. That's the starting point: to understand and to look for opportunities. But before you jump in, stop. Take a walk outside, take some deep breaths, do whatever your version of breaking away is, of allowing things to settle in your head, and get to a place where you can bring fresh eyes to the process.

Starting where Jerry Seinfeld did at the beginning of all of his bits, asking "Have you ever wondered why people do the things they do the way they do them . . . ?" is a form of fresh eyes that includes empathy, curiosity, and seeing clearly what others don't. Once you've cleaned your glasses thus, you can see more sharply what is in front of you, around the corner, and down the road.

Each of the chapters that follow is about looking at the market through different lenses from different perspectives—because the best opportunities are not those in front of your nose. On this, LVMH's group managing director, Antonio Belloni, has some gems of wisdom to offer.

I keep this picture in my mind of the established market, which I see like a table. All the existing players are sitting at the table and used to doing things in a certain way. They know how the game is played. They are optimizing, not reinventing. But standing above the table with a different perspective are a number of startups. They have not been at this table, so they don't know the "rules." These startups are in a position to look at lots of tables and can come up with a different perspective, a fresh mind. They can often find pain points or points of friction or other, often easier, ways of doing things that the players at the table don't see or have learned to accept as just the way things are.[9]

The market is sort of like a game of football or baseball. There are so many points of view from which it can be seen and understood: offense, defense, umps, fans, commentators, TV viewers at home. How do you get into each of those spots to see it all? The idea of the lenses is to help you broaden your perspective and see things that others are missing.

Belloni offers a great, albeit counterintuitive, hint: "It's easier for the nonincumbent, for the people outside of the market, to see what needs to be seen. To think with that mentality, you have to cultivate doubt, much more than certainties, in your people."[10] It is with this sense of doubt that you can bring a fresh mind to seeing things through the many lenses I will provide here.

FOCUS IN & DRILL DOWN

When you teach someone how to throw a baseball, you tell them to look where they want the ball to go, step toward where they want the ball to go, and then throw the ball where they want it to go. To the novice thrower, this can sound frustratingly uninstructive. So, too, is the simple complexity that is viewing your business in a way that narrows your perspective to one that can provide an experience that is specific, unique, and superior to all the others.

The strongest brands have a clear focus on what they do, what they want to stand for, and to whom they can provide it, and they offer what they do in the same way and with the same quality every time they do it. The clearer the focus, the stronger the brand. Companies that try to veer off the path—getting into what they consider collateral offerings—often get into trouble. Consumers are smart enough to question the connection. A key factor in brand success is to concentrate on what you do and do it well.

As *New York Times* columnist Tom Friedman once said to me in a conversation a few years back, "Average is over." In this hyper-connected world, "good enough" is no longer enough. Taking this one step further, relative to seeing new opportunities, consider how to "unbundle" one particular dimension of an experience, and then become the expert in that area. This is a lens that has provided success to a number of market innovators.

And it often starts with standing up and moving from behind your desk, putting down your phone, and looking away from your screens. You have to exist in the world where you want to succeed. If you don't know what it's like to shop at a supermarket, you are unlikely to understand how to create an experience that will make your supermarket do something that no one else does. All of this is easier said than done, of course. When Friedman and I talked about how the idea for his book *Thank You for Being Late* originated, he told me that he never minded if one of his appointments ran late and he was left waiting in reception for longer than expected. He always saw this as a gift of unstructured time in a space that he hadn't chosen, and it's where he's had some of his best ideas or come to an idea for a solution to a previously intractable problem.

TOO BUSY TO SEE WHAT WE NEED TO SEE

We all have our version of missing things because we're too busy to see them. In my younger days, I went out for a run on most mornings. Let me be clear: I had no great ambitions or quests for a personal best. I ran not too far, two or three miles, and I ran them not that quickly (though I will keep my dignity intact and not share my pace). While I would make my way around Central Park's reservoir, I'd enjoy the view, the air, the music playing through my headphones—and it was in those moments that I had some of my best ideas. Challenges that felt impossible would unravel at a slow, incremental pace the way a tangled knot can be addressed one bit of tangle at a time. This was the kind of thinking I could never do sitting at my desk, no matter how clear my mind was and no matter how on top of my inbox I managed to be.

It isn't a secret that we all, to some degree, suffer now from some version of too-busy syndrome. We all find ourselves believing that if we are doing two things, even three, at a time, we are more productive. Those of us in the corporate world overschedule ourselves, and we do so deliberately. In my previous book, *Shift Ahead*, I mention a meeting I had with then-CMO of Facebook, Gary Briggs. He talked about how, if you were working on a priority project, you got what was called the "Hall Pass," which would allow you to clear your calendar of most meetings in order to fully dive into and focus on a project that took you outside of your everyday tasks.

For my generation, it used to be that if you wanted to see what was going on outside of your immediate, corporate existence, you could just turn on the television. There before you would be ads for all sorts of products and services, certainly any about which you would want to be aware. And that viewing did offer some sense of what was going on in the world, which is how senior management would look at things. When I was at Unilever it was "Did you see that ad that Colgate just ran for a new product? We've got to get going on something here." At a different gig, it was "Did you see what I just saw on television last night? Look what they're doing in the insurance category."

STEP OUTSIDE OF YOUR BUBBLE

The world of media no longer allows you to simply watch television to get a full sense of things, as anyone over the age of fifty knows. The list of offerings is dictated by an algorithm driven by what I click on and watch.

My demographics, in every sense of the word, narrow the world to what someone out there thinks a man of my age, of my socioeconomic bracket, of my region, of my profession, of my predilections wants to see. And I'm not casting aspersions on their accuracy. This is about how my, your, everyone's experience is a curated view crafted on our behalf, unbeknownst to us. The effect is that I am unable, without real effort, to identify what I or companies for whom I consult might want to do, offer, or bring to the world—because my own perspective is so siloed.

This was made as clear as the sky is blue when I was in Ann Arbor, Michigan, speaking to a marketing class at the Ross School of Business. As is my usual, I found my way to the Graduate Hotel gym's treadmill. Watching the morning news on my phone, I was presented with ads for companies and products I had never heard of. It wasn't that I lived an ad-free life. Even in the age of streaming, I still use the ad-supported version of Hulu, I watch plenty of sports, and I get at least 50 percent of my news from live (not written) sources. I see advertising—or so I thought. What I was in the process of learning firsthand was the extent to which my existence, my exposure to the world and all that happens in it, has been slowly but surely (or, not so slowly) whittled away such that what I know of the world is a highly curated, narrow range, dictated not by me but by what my viewing and scrolling habits suggest about me. As someone who fancies myself aware of what is going on, this was startling.

So there it was. I was about to speak to a class at the University of Michigan and was staying at a hotel on campus—and as a result, the advertising directed at me was incredibly different from what I saw when the screen thought I was a sixty-something white guy on the Upper East Side of Manhattan. I began to wonder: How could I step out of my bubble? I turned to my media partner at Metaforce, Bill Heilman. I asked him if he could configure my phone and home TV so it would think I was different people, in different places, with different interests, vulnerable to different clickbait, and every other metric I could think of.

What Bill explained to me was fascinating. This less-curated view is only the tip of what is out there, unseen by me unless I make a concerted effort. "As marketers, we always talk about trying to walk in the shoes of the consumer, and we've traditionally done this with ethnographic research, going into people's homes and seeing what they use and how they use it. But what I think is more interesting is what you might learn by creating different personas and starting to look at things through the world of these different consumers firsthand," Bill said.[1] Browsing behavior dictated by an entirely different personal profile would result in a plethora of views into worlds you can't otherwise see.

"If I, Bill, like to buy fragrances, which I do, I will spend time on a site like Kilian," Bill continued. "Soon, when I go through Google, I will start seeing fragrance-related advertising. I might even see an ad for a laundry detergent that is fragrance oriented. The next step, then, is to go to different platforms, disguise as various members of your potential audience, with different anchors (my anchor being fragrances), and see where this leads Google and other targeted advertising to go."[2] This allows you to step outside of these highly curated silos in which we all live (with varying degrees of awareness) and see the world from as many angles as possible.

I would argue that you need Facebook's "Hall Pass," and you need to stop using curated advertising to be able to spot the obvious. You need to get out of the office, shake up your routine, and step away from your weekly, daily, and multiple-times-a-day meetings. If you are always in back-to-back meetings and back-to-back calls, scanning lots of data, and absorbing one-pagers, you'll be unable to see the forest for the trees.

When the Walkman Was the It Thing

Taken to the next level, we can see companies that have successfully drilled down to the heart of an issue or service and made it not just their core but their entire business. Many of them seem obvious and unworthy of note, so ingrained are their ideas, but there was a time before they existed. And that "before time" exists for other services, products, and problems unsolved; this is where you come in.

You could be the person who does their own version of what Sony did in 1979 with the Walkman those many, many years ago, which was a perfect example of focusing in. As Steven Fuld, senior vice president of marketing at Sony, told me, "The Walkman was positioned to give the listener control in their life."[3] Sony produced a product that reduced to its essence what someone would need to have music playing no matter where they were.

The original Walkman had no radio, no bells and whistles; it was a cassette player with the attendant buttons (play, fast-forward, reverse) and a single port into which a single pair of headphones plugged. The sound quality was previously only available in your den sitting in front of large speakers connected to a collection of large electronic components. Sony understood that this was more than a new product launch. It was selling a new experience to anyone who wanted to know what it was like to walk out on the street, on the treadmill, or into a subway car and have their favorite song playing in their head. It may be hard to recall, but there was a time before 1979 when such a thing simply did not exist. At that time, music played into an entire room, had to be for the ears of everyone within listening distance, and was confined to those spaces where a music source, wires, an outlet, and speakers could be found.

In order to paint the picture as vividly as possible, Sony sent a woman by the name of Maki Kumagai out into NYC during the summer of 1978 to just walk around wearing a Walkman. Kumagai was the original influencer/ guerilla marketer.

The original intent of the product was to show that music could be mobile and controlled by the individual listener. Commuting to and from work or school, taking a walk, or running errands, the sounds that previously only existed at home—where you could play your cassette tapes or albums and hear them through speakers that were built to stay put—could now live in your pocket. As Fuld describes it,

> Sony took what they did, [creating] devices for home entertainment, and drilled down to its essence to identify an aspect of that experience they could offer their customers in a form that was portable and pocket-sized. They made it as small as they could, surrounding the space into which the cassette went with just enough mechanics and space for batteries to allow it to run. In this way, they showed the extent to which this control was available to anyone willing to purchase a Walkman.[4]

Talk about changing the consumer experience!

One of my favorite ads of all time is one Sony ran in 1988 (which you can find by searching "Sony 1988 Walkman ad" on YouTube), for which the company won art direction awards, that shows a monkey standing at a beautiful vista by the ocean, holding a Walkman, with the headphones in its ears, as a well-known opera aria plays. The voiceover tells us that the Walkman has forever changed the way we listen to music—and it was not speaking hyperbolically. By drilling down into the essence of its product—putting sound in the ears of people on the move—Sony helped create a society where words, music, news, and entertainment of all mediums travel with us.

Make Your Name Your Purpose: 1–800 Contacts and So Much More

You can be the source of the idea that is the 1-800 Contacts of your world. In 1995, Jonathan C. Coon and John F. Nichols founded the company from their idea to get a product that has daily use into the daily-life experience of everyone who wears them (like myself). Before them, I would get my contacts when I visited my optometrist to have my eyes checked. And then, when I would run out, I would drive back to that office and pick up more of them. Sometimes they would mail them to me. It was time consuming, it had to be done at very specific business hours, and I was highly involved in the process. But back then, that was how and where you got contacts. The name and concept for 1-800 Contacts combined the point of contact (a phone number, in those pre-internet days) with how to be the first thought when you think of contact lenses: the toll-free number that sticks in your head whether you want it to or not.

They weren't the first to notice that people who wear contacts need a steady supply of them. They weren't the first ones to imagine that a toll-free way of ordering them would be a good idea. But they were the ones to create a contact lens–buying experience. They did this by drawing the line between the need (a consistent, reliable, and easy source of a disposable product that is used every day), the problem (how to make fulfilling this need take up as little time and thought as possible), and how to be the one more people would turn to for the solution (is there any easier way to recall where you can get your contacts than "1-800 Contacts," which provides the information for both what to dial and what you'll buy when they pick up on the other end?). They retained their customers by offering the service they provided consistently and by offering a wide range of choices, both of which are easier to do when you focus in and do one thing very well.

But ultimately, when you find yourself in a similar place to where they were in 1995 and can solve a very specific problem and execute that solution better because you are so focused on it and only it, you will likely succeed in business more so than the competition because this may be too far for most others to go. Many, many people have the same idea at the same time in many, many businesses, but the ones that succeed are the ones that execute best. And if your business is really focused—in this case, selling contact lenses and only contact lenses—you're more likely to be able to stock the right amounts of product, buy them at a better price, and ship them faster. By choosing the narrow area that you are going to do better than anyone else and understanding it more fully than others could aspire to, the machine you build will be superior to that of those trying to do a wider range of things for a more varied group of people or issues.

To do so, you need to start at the beginning. For pre-internet contacts purchasing, that meant getting people to memorize the company name and phone number—the first point of contact with consumers. By arriving at "1-800 Contacts," the founders removed the friction of name recognition and contact-lens information in one fell swoop. Their success begat other similarly mnemonic businesses, like 1-800-GOT-JUNK?, 1-800-Flowers .com, PetMeds, and so many others that are no doubt going through your mind as I mention these.

Another example of focusing in of this kind—where you pinpoint one thing in a larger market that you know you can do, do well, and execute smoothly and for which there is an identifiable market by creating a new experience for a known service—is the strategic use of virtual learning.

Remote teaching existed before the pandemic, but it has been fine-tuned throughout and since. When I was telling Fuld about this book, he told me about his daughter's interest in learning Mandarin. Finding someone to work with her remotely (due to the pandemic) wasn't difficult; there was a plethora of options that ranged from the basic to the highly bespoke. But when they discovered how easily they could hire and work with a teacher *in China*, the decision was clear. This teacher realized that once their overseas audience was remote-ready, the way to be the clear choice was to use the newly defined reality (going remote) to their advantage. Offering Mandarin lessons while also providing culture and context, not to mention dialect and modern slang, set them apart from US-based teachers. This is another form of focusing in on what you do, do well, and do in a way that is different from what others do and making the consumer experience that much more meaningful. This is how you differentiate yourself.

The Perfect Blowout and Only the Perfect Blowout: Drybar

Drybar is a great example of a service version of 1-800 Contacts's concept: take one aspect of a service and drill it down to offer a single service, in all its permutations, and offer it with a consistently excellent execution, and you have yourself a focused-in success. As more and more women included blowouts in their weekly (or more frequent) routines, salons that offered cuts, color, facials, nails, and so on tried to keep up with demand. But stylists who cut and colored were not always available to do what was once the final step of a full appointment and not the step a customer necessarily paid for separately.

Drybar changed all of that. It started with the problem: How can we offer blowout services in a space that is dedicated to that service, rather than trying to cram it in along the edges of a preexisting salon ecosystem? If you were lucky, the place where you got your hair cut knew how to straighten your hair in a way that would last for a day or two. If you were lucky, the way they did it was the way that looked good on you. And, if you were extra lucky, they could find a stylist willing to put aside the more lucrative cut-and-color appointment to provide the service to you.

A stand-alone business was the solution. Make that business one where the only service offered is styling hair. Drybar said, Let's identify all the many ways people like to have their hair styled. Let's create products that will make the effect of those different variations as close to ideal as possible, far exceeding what anyone might be able to do themselves or even have done by the random stylist in a normal salon. We'll train stylists to perform the various types of styling in such a way that customers will know that no matter which Drybar they turn to—the one near home, near work, near their gym—they will achieve the same look no matter who is behind their chair. More importantly, all of this will be broadly available at Drybar because this is what Drybar will do.

When you focus in, understand what is not being offered now, and think through your service at such a granular level, the product that results will be one that redefines the service itself.

A CLOSER LOOK: WHEN IT'S EASIER TO START THE COMPANY THAN BOOK A MEETING TO TALK ABOUT IT: CALENDLY

Technology and work have long been friends (or frenemies, depending on who is talking). The pandemic has moved the dial with a speed that could take your breath away. Ensuring that the future of work allows for people to work in the office, from home, or in some hybrid version has resulted in massive improvements in the world of cloud services, communications, and productivity apps. Those who identified specific aspects of work life that hold the distinction for both bogging down productivity and revealing potential for improvements have found success in ways they could not have imagined before 2020. Calendly is one of those who went narrow and won big.

The Endless Patience and Hours of Coordination

When I worked in corporate America, I counted myself among the lucky for any number of reasons, but the top of that list was Leonie Derry. She offered me phenomenal support for many, many years at Landor Associates. I appreciated her enormously and made sure she knew it. I could walk by her desk and say, "I need a meeting with Bill, Tom, and Susan in the next day, and it will last about an hour." And then, a couple of hours later, I would say, "My client needs a conference call with me and Rob, but I also want the creative director there, too." This would happen many times throughout the day, every day. And these meetings and calls and events just happened. Leonie knew all the players, so I didn't need to explain or extemporize beyond my initial quip. She knew I preferred longer meetings in the morning, and she knew how long the longest meeting could be. She knew when I preferred to have meals when the conversation was difficult and where I had my version of Happy Meals. I didn't think much about it, not for a long time—until I became an entrepreneur.

It wasn't until I shifted to the life of the entrepreneur and money from my own pocket, rather than from a large corporate budget, paying for the time of my assistant that I realized how much time was spent on coordinating my meetings. I had initially failed to understand all of what was involved in coordinating meeting and schedules, but I learned pretty quickly. Every plan started the clock on an excruciating round-robin of "I can do this day, I can do that time, but I can't eat that food, and I never meet on Tuesdays." My entrepreneurial journey was suddenly paved with details and minutiae I never even knew existed. And when every dime is *your* dime, the expression "time is money" takes on new meaning. I needed time to be used efficiently. All time: mine, that of those who worked for me, everyone's time. Every time one thing on my schedule shifted, it was like a house of cards—it all came down. Rebuilding it took even more time. What existed with pen and paper had to, by necessity, move to the screen—but deciding how, where, and which platform took time that, while well spent, verged on becoming another time suck. My life was a life of meetings. All I did was figure out how to gather one group of people in order to figure out together how best to solve a problem for another group of people. My calendar was my life.

A User Interface That Understood Me

Then, one day, the clouds parted and light shone down when someone sent me a Calendly link. From a focusing-in perspective, the story of Calendly is one that rises above the plethora of plan-making, digital calendar–linked ways to schedule a meeting. You would think Google or Microsoft or Apple would and could have solved the issue a long time ago. But their focus wasn't on addressing the issue of planning *what* goes on the calendar; they were busy figuring out how best to replace paper calendars. Once they did this, they failed to zoom out and focus on the elephant in the room, one that was there with paper and was exacerbated on the screen: making the event happen with the people you wanted to include in attendance. Calendly is a story about doing one thing, doing it well, doing it better than others, and rising above the pack because you've focused in.

A startup, Calendly is a popular cloud-based service that workers can use to set up and confirm meeting times with others. This is a process that, even when everyone is working in the same space, poses difficulties. Put those bodies in multiple places (and even time zones), and you have challenges that could defy even the most organized of souls. The beauty of this freemium software-as-service is its simplicity. The platform offers a quick way to manage open spaces in your calendar, which allows others to know when you are free and book your time, simultaneously updating connected Google and Microsoft Outlook calendars. Those to whom you send your Calendly link can use Calendly themselves to identify the empty slots in their own calendar that align with yours. The user interface is so seamless and smooth, it's hard to imagine why or how anyone would try to do it differently. There are extra services that make the platform the go-to it has so quickly become, including the ability to pay for a service when the appointment isn't a business meeting but rather, say, a yoga class. The more events, integrations, and features, the greater the argument to move from the free to the premium to the pro versions. And every time a user has a good experience booking with someone through the service, a new user is born. In return, the more a user relies on it as the easiest way to organize their time, the more solid their loyalty to the platform becomes. All because a specific need was narrowly, and fully, addressed.

Calendly created a user interface so seamless and smooth it's hard to imagine why or how anyone would try to do it differently. The platform offers an efficient way to book open slots in your calendar, which allows those to whom you send your Calendly link to use Calendly to identify those empty slots in their calendar which align with yours. As work and life has moved into the remote realm, all of the encounters that used to happen organically now need to be scheduled intentionally. In other words, if everyone is in their respective homes, there is no chance that most of any given department will find themselves in the break room and arrange for a last-minute sit-down over the day's recently emerged challenge. Everything that once happened by popping into another person's office (teacher-student meetings are a great example) now needs to be scheduled in advance. Fewer people are in their offices, so the likelihood of catching someone on the phone is slim; now, the therapist appointment is booked through Calendly, as are dinner parties.

We Solve Our Own Problems Better Than Anyone Else Can

Tope Awotona was born in Lagos, Nigeria, to a pharmacist mother and a father who worked at Unilever. After finishing high school at the age of fifteen, he studied business at the University of Georgia, specializing in management information systems, after which he worked in the same field at both IBM and EMC. He landed on the idea for Calendly after a few other entrepreneurial ideas came to naught in the ensuing years. In fact, one of the frustrations he encountered when trying to establish the viability of his ideas was the difficulty of bringing together the people needed for the conversation.

He started Calendly in 2013 and shifted operations to Ukraine in 2014. He was no software engineer, and he put up personal equity rather than relying on venture money; he truly bootstrapped his way to profitability. To some extent, his vision precluded anyone rushing toward him waving money. And he didn't do a lot to raise Calendly's profile or seek attention. He was hardly the first person to try developing scheduling software—far from it. But from the start, Calendly was conceived as something a user could use with ease, born out of Awotona's own frustration in trying to set up meetings while working at tech companies like Dell EMC.

There, he had been a sales guy. Not just any sales guy, but a software sales guy. To make the sale, you didn't meet with and get one person on board. It required many different people from many different parts of a given company to meet, to understand the product, and to sign on to use it. In today's business world, where bringing an idea or project to fruition requires the involvement and input of a wide range of voices, the logistics of bringing those minds together—literally—is an obvious barrier to progress. Awotona set out to solve a problem he faced personally, and that explains a good bit of his success. His frustration was deeply felt and specifically understood. That's when he got to work. What he did, he did well, with a focus that led to an outcome that defied the Tech Giants—the Microsofts, the Googles, the Apples. Why? How? Because he started with empathy. As he told Guy Raz, he started by "signing up for every single product that existed on the market and deconstructing them, just tearing them apart."[5]

He really needed what he ultimately created. "I felt like I had a calling to do this right for a number of reasons. I spent all my life in sales, and I really understood. I thought I knew a lot about meetings and media etiquette and what works and what doesn't work."[6] He knew firsthand the challenges created by the limitations of software when it came to multiple people trying to collaboratively meet. He knew that those challenges took bites out of his bottom line, his ability to conduct his business. From start to finish, Calendly came to be something that responded to what Awotona wanted for himself and what he wanted to offer to others. It has a free initial-user level, and to use it is to share it. In other words, its user interface has spreading the word baked into it because it asks that both sender and recipient sign in.

What Is True Customer Centricity?

I am reminded of something marketing professor Kevin Keller once told me. One of the most common things you hear from businesses today is how customer-centric they are. But according to Keller (and some reasonable observation), most are not. As Keller asks, "What do you mean by that, and how do you express this mindset?"[7] To truly embody customer centricity, you have to bring empathy to the party. "You have to learn how to see through their eyes; you have to know how to walk in their shoes. That's when you start talking about customer centricity. That's when you're not looking just to spreadsheets—you are imagining real, live humans interacting with what you do or sell."[8] This is not what most companies are doing, and it shows.

Customer centricity's effect is so broad, it has even given rise to debates about etiquette. Is it rude to make someone choose a time based on your current calendar openings? Is sending a link rather than an extended "How do you feel about meeting on Tuesday at three?" message suggesting that my time is more important than that of the person to whom I'm sending the link?

When Awotona explored the scheduling options available as an entrepreneur, he found that most were not up to the task of coordinating large numbers of people (say, ten to twenty) for a single commitment, and those that even tried wanted a commitment (subscription) up front. He speaks of being inspired by Dropbox's cloud-based approach, which allows different users to use the same platform as their individual setup dictates.

Once the viability of the scheduling was established, he looked for ways to distinguish what the platform offered while remaining true to its very specific purpose: scheduling an event for a time that made it easy for those who were needed to attend and for those who wanted to attend to do so. As a result, the ability to pay the attendant fees, say, for an event was folded in, making it easier for people to set up recurring events while still maintaining the ability to edit the specifics of any one gathering, and so forth. Awotona wanted to offer services that made a given meeting better, more efficient, and easier to schedule, with follow-up and simple ways to set things up to recur as needed. He was very clear in wanting to stay in his own lane—he had no interest in the meetings themselves. He was not taking on Zoom or any other platform or service that hosted a gathering. He stayed focused.

A CLOSER LOOK: A SPACE WHERE VILLAGES GATHER ISN'T EASY TO BUILD: DISCORD

Discord started as a way to solve a problem the founders themselves faced as users: how to communicate with friends around the world while playing video games online. Ever since they were kids, Jason Citron and Stan Vishnevskiy both loved video games and the connections they made with other players. Their voice- and text-communication app and digital distribution system, Discord, was released on May 13, 2015, and was ranked third in CNBC's 2021 Disruptor 50, which lists companies leading the pace of technological change. While there has always been a vast

number of ways, platforms, software, and devices in and on which people
of like minds can go to exchange ideas, images, videos, and such, Discord understood that there was a narrower and more specific need in the
realm of gaming, and it stepped up to provide it. Even the name spoke
to the focus in its intent. After considering other options, the company
was called "Discord" because the word had something to do with talking,
sounded cool, was easily pronounceable, was memorable, and had an
available domain name.

The founders' initial focus was extremely narrow: gamers. What did
gamers need to do? They needed to be able to play together in real time;
they wanted to share thoughts, pictures, and videos about what they were
doing (and whatever else they were thinking about); and they were not
going to take kindly to an algorithm trying to decide the who, what, and
where of the content they were going to see. What today is a text, voice,
and video-chat platform with more than 140 million active users and nine-
teen million active servers started out by making it possible for the already
technologically comfortable to settle in and commune with those they
chose. Each individually run group is called a server; for each server, there
is a moderator and a private user group; and, within that circle, the rules
of conduct, play, and otherwise are determined by the person who established the server.

Understand What Has Not Been Done and Do It

What might look to the non-Discord user like a service that replicates what
exists in so many other forms is in fact wonderfully unique in its universe.
Because of the focus brought to what it is there to achieve, it simply hops
over what causes so many of the other platforms to stumble. Each server
is, for all intents and purposes, an online community unto itself; what
works for one community doesn't work for another. Rules and parameters are determined by what is needed or wanted, with no need to oblige

one community to make sacrifices or accommodations in order to allow another group to function with autonomy. Within a server, real-time talk and video can happen, and different users can have customized roles, so much so that Discord's original intent—to be a space where gamers could livestream and chat—has grown far beyond that to incorporate as many types of users as there are communities of humans.

At the most fundamental level, Discord understood that its users would accept nothing short of an opt-in structure. The technology was understood by the initial users in a way that made this patently clear, starting with the founders. In Discord, no algorithm determines who and what you hear. Most of the groupings of users are private, created to enable the dissemination of regular and controlled content to the users with whom you choose to engage. And if you do choose to engage, there is nothing you can't do or share. You can play a game, post code, share videos, speak on audio or video conferences, as well as share your screen. You can engage with a massive community of others, should you choose to. By focusing in on what it is about social platforms that a particular kind of user wants, Discord's founders created a space that parents are far more comfortable allowing their thirteen-year-olds to enter (an entirely opt-in, private-setting community with no chance of unwanted stranger interaction but a terrific space in which friends can gather remotely) and that adult users appreciate because they can control how much or little they wish to interact with the outside world.

At its essence, Discord created an experience that was unique within a world of many platforms. The experience was defined by founders who lived the experience they wanted to improve, and that always makes for a more successful outcome, one that we see echoed throughout successful business case studies. Its growth, exponential and still on the rise, is predicated on its appeal and accessibility to those outside of the gaming community, though this wasn't always the case.

Broaden Your Audience Without Diluting the Power of Your Product

The developers may not have initially shown much interest in non-gaming users, but those users were always there. In 2020, focus groups revealed the extent to which this was the case. People organizing hobby groups, study groups, and lessons for entirely recreational purposes were all present on the platform, but they were struggling to make full and easy use of it because of the preponderance of gaming symbols and argot. In response, a redesign created a platform that would appeal to a broader audience without losing its original one. And the timing turned out to be good because the pandemic led a lot of people to stay home and create their social lives online.

The experience that Discord originally provided—one that gave gamers all they might need to play, talk about their play, and show off how well they've played—was expanded to include others for whom the experience of talking, sharing, and interacting with one another online had suddenly become a significant part of their lives. Discord accomplished what it did by staying committed to improving the experience it provided for as many people as wanted to join it. Discord did not try to become something else; it just did what it did better than everyone else did. Interestingly, what it does so well is a combination of what others do with less-than-stellar success. It offers a social-media space (like Facebook and Instagram), an online community forum (Reddit), and a video/audio calling tool (Zoom), and it brings them together without many of the difficulties those other spaces face. And it avoided many of the pitfalls it might have faced otherwise—the developers kept it as a web-browser launch, so there was never an issue of different versions of the software working with some better than with others. People could just open the site, click, and proceed to engage.

Through Discord, users create communities they want to play, talk, and share in with technological interfaces that are consistently superior because they are created by the kinds of people whose expectations are highest. How, then, does Discord produce income, given its no-ads policy? By offering premium services—services offered at a high enough quality and that improve the original experience by a great enough margin to make it worthwhile for those who use it. When Discord tried to step out of its lane and, for example, monetize by selling games, it did not go well. But when it focused on what it does best and remembered that it does it better than anyone else can, Discord found success to an undisputed degree.

A CLOSER LOOK: YOU SHOULDN'T HAVE TO HAVE BUCKETS OF MONEY TO PLAY THE STOCK MARKET: ROBINHOOD

In keeping with the name, the founders of Robinhood focused in on what the "haves" had and what was being denied to the "have nots." The story of Robinhood is of two people identifying an arena that is vital to financial health and yet was steeped with barricades keeping a large number of people from participating. They sought to explicitly democratize an experience, making it accessible to all, by focusing their service on the ways in which someone who doesn't have two million dollars, or even two thousand, to play with can still invest in the stock market.

When I talked about Robinhood with Guy Raz, he made an interesting observation:

> With a product like Robinhood, they didn't invent e-trading—they didn't even invent trading on an app, which you could have already done through E-trade and in other products. They amplified it and innovated in other ways and forced other competitors to follow by creating a very, very easy-to-use and intuitive interface. And they removed so much friction from the process, they tapped into

something that clearly younger consumers under the age of, let's say, thirty-five, wanted. As with most services and products that change behavior, I think much of the products that are doing that now are driven by younger consumers.[9]

The "they" in question are Vlad Tenev and Baiju Bhatt, who went to Stanford together but couldn't imagine being the math professors they seemed in line to become. Living in Brooklyn, they built two finance companies, selling trading software to hedge funds, all the while seeing with increasing clarity the reality of the stock market.

First, they saw that technology had allowed computers and algorithms to trade faster than humans could. The faster you trade, the faster you are able to find the gap between selling the stock at one price and selling it at a price infinitesimally lower than the one to be had a moment ago. With that vantage point, you can quickly buy low and sell high.

And then there was the other truth about who got to play in the stock-market sandbox in the first place—and the extent to which the stock market was built to support that kind of user and keep out the others. To start, they couldn't help but notice that while it cost Wall Street investment firms little to nothing to trade stocks and there was no inherent reason for a minimum to buy a stock, there were significant financial barriers and fees to entering into the process for individuals. Buying a publicly traded stock, these two thought, should be as accessible as the voting booth. So they focused on the users and asked why it couldn't be. If big Wall Street firms pay nothing to trade, they shouldn't charge clients fees to do so. Tenev and Bhatt then shifted their focus to building products that would improve access for everyone, not just those with significant financial assets. They developed Robinhood in 2013 and launched the app in 2015 with the focused aim of encouraging anyone and everyone to participate in the financial systems that rule our world.

Throw Open the Doors of Finance and Let the People In

Influenced by the Occupy Wall Street movement of 2011, Tenev and Bhatt saw the ease with which someone with a chunk of money, knowledge, and access to the stock market could make money off of it. Their understanding of the market allowed them to see the enormous benefits of taking milliseconds out of trades and finding faster and faster analytics, and in this they saw all the potential of a moneymaking scenario. What they also saw was the fact that the barriers to access were artificially formed to keep those with less from having more. They saw that the fees charged by firms were based on no actual cost to those firms. They wanted to make trading free—since the market was, in fact, free.

Having made it free, they also made it possible for those just starting out to make their trades with the same ease with which they might, say, post on Instagram. In fact, moving from Instagram to Reddit to Robinhood was the most natural thing in the world, and that is exactly how it was used. Not only could you execute a buy on your phone while waiting for a coffee, but you could also buy one share or just a fraction of a share—and the gamification of the process, the democratization of the world-controlling stock market, was suddenly in the hands of those kept on the outside for so long.

The focus these founders put on not just opening the doors but also on inviting a very specific demographic in showed an even more fine-tuned understanding of their mission that led to the success they achieved. This focus was about taking original technology that made free trade as well as fractional stock purchases possible; plus, they pitched it to a generation already primed and ready for a gamified system. Robinhood's users were already attached to their phones and already convinced that they were able to gather information and apply it in a valuable way.

The democratization—the "Robinhood" of it all—took the adage that you had to be rich and have access to play the market and said, quite simply, "No." And there was a delicious amount of creative marketing that put it all together, with the familiar Robinhood feather reinforcing the idea, already culturally steeped, that anyone with a phone had the power, should they decide to use it.

Invite the Young, for They Will Be Inheriting What Is Left Behind

A generation that knows they have and will be left holding the bag with a host of crises—financial, environmental, political—believes it has the answers. As easily as they can Venmo a friend for their half of a burrito, they can now buy a fraction of a stock. And, as they saw with the GameStop short squeeze and other incidents, those fractions can add up to real power. Making things free is the ultimate form of removing friction.

Technology has made possible this kind of increased access to spaces previously limited to a select few. Apple is one of the larger players moving the world in that direction, though the access it creates is generally about ease of use. Though personal computing once remained the domain of those with technological comfort, Apple approaches everything with an eye on design and user interface. Buying a new computer, migrating information from one device to another, and introducing new software has all been made effortless—and for those who want more, Apple offers support by people with a profound and deep knowledge of everything about its devices and technology.

For most, and for a long time, the idea of playing the stock market was one available only to the wealthy. Specifically, you needed enough to be worth the time of brokers who, by and large, prefer to work with those with significant resources. For those just starting out at their first "adult job"—who are rightfully proud to be thinking about saving and making their savings grow—this was a stumbling block that stood between them and a future toward which they wished to save. Robinhood saw this and was created from this kernel of understanding.

Invite the Once Excluded

Robinhood identified the need, a fairly obvious one once it was stated aloud: there was a wide-ranging population of people out there with finite amounts of money who nevertheless wanted to put some of it into the stock market. This is a way to grow your money, one of few available to those who have no hope of playing with larger entities like real estate or other large-cap investments. Robinhood identified the problem and arrived at a way to be the conduit through which these heretofore unlikely investors could join the party. It sought to democratize investing, and it went after those most actively pursuing access: millennials. Robinhood met the millennials where they spend their time—on their phones—and made it easy. No need to open a brokerage account at Merrill Lynch, where you meet minimums, meet with a broker, and play broadly and widely. You can do it while waiting for your Starbucks half-caf Frappuccino with a drizzle and shot. Robinhood is a truly classic case of focusing in and building a product narrowly with a deep understanding of both what you do (create access to stocks) and the audience best suited to avail themselves of your service or product (millennials and those with more limited funds and a deep comfort in performing transactions on the same device on which they scroll through Instagram).

Investments took the form of individual buys of specific stocks. You could scroll through Instagram and Twitter, gather some facts to lead you to believe a particular (publicly traded) company is doing something interesting in a way that could be remuneratively forthcoming, and all you'd have to do is pause your game and touch a different icon on your home screen. And voilà—all of a sudden, everybody could invest and gamify the market, with all the incumbent pros and cons. Most importantly, as Raz pointed out to me when we talked about Robinhood, by bringing the stock market to young people in the space where they already spent their time, Robinhood not only opened the doors to the previously excluded; it also encouraged a habit and expectation of involvement in their own wealth creation earlier and with the potential for long-term effect. "Traditionally, the way most people have created wealth is by doing it slowly, putting it into an index fund and watching it grow. It's a different perception now about how to create wealth. I don't know if it's correct, but it's certainly interesting. It changes the way people invest and behave with money."[10] How Robinhood did this was, as Raz so accurately said later, by creating "a product that was tactile, personal, an extension of ourselves, of our bodies." Robinhood forced other platforms to mimic the experience it created in order to keep doing what they had already been doing. "They removed so much friction from the process; they tapped into something that, clearly, younger consumers wanted."[11]

The Young Taking Ownership

And tapped they have done. According to a 2021 study, of Gen Z and millennial investors (those aged eighteen to forty), Robinhood was the most-used investing app. Thirty-seven percent of all respondents reported using Robinhood in the past month—more specifically, 40 percent of Gen Z investors (ages eighteen to twenty-four) and 36 percent of millennials (ages twenty-five to forty)[12]—with no other app achieving that level of market saturation. The ease with which the Robinhood app integrates into the way young generations gather information speaks to this success: 91 percent of Gen Z respondents reported using social media as a source of information for investing above any other source.[13] That said, Robinhood investors are unique in their use of traditional investing websites and SEC filings, more than those who use other apps.

When you change consumer behavior, it stops being about the product (there are hundreds of ways to buy stocks), and it becomes entirely about the experience. Robinhood is entirely focused on a segment of business, and it drills down on it relentlessly: it's all about buying stocks, doing so without minimums and fees, and doing so on your phone. The act of buying and selling stocks isn't new. Others have offered different fee structures. The difference: experience—the ability to access the investing world in real time (and out in the world, like waiting in line at the movies) that was once closed off. In pondering the degree to which this is so much a shift in experience (versus a new service or product being offered), Raz pointed out to me how much this is becoming more and more the norm. "The vast majority of people I've had on the show are creating interesting businesses, they're innovating, but they're building on what's there," he said. "Even the biggest of innovators are building on what's there, but the vast majority are businesses that are making minor modifications of existing products and services," with an emphasis on who they are selling to and what it's like when the product is brought into use.

The motivation that differentiated Robinhood was a belief that the financial marketplace was inherently corrupt and deliberately closed off to outsiders (the majority) and that it was deeply unfair that only a few were given the opportunity to avail themselves of the profits the markets generated. Unlike the protest movements of lore, Robinhood's mission, according to Bhatt, included an affirmative slant. This wasn't about taking down capitalism—it was about bringing the opportunity to make money in this very capitalistic system to more people with a wider range of resources. The belief that there were people who wanted in but couldn't find the door was at the heart of what made this idea so unusual and so successful.

Robinhood took a group that was previously uninterested in and unengaged with the stock market and made that statement untrue. It recognized that the disenfranchisement was not a result of an active disinterest so much as it was a reflection of an understandable belief that the stock market was unavailable, not a part of the world in which the young could partake. Despite an understanding that the stock market dictated so much of life as they knew it, the financial markets had deliberately framed themselves as for a narrowly defined elite. With the easy user interface and a proclamation to "democratize finance for all," Robinhood's app spoke in a way that made sense and was heard. It took a basic fact—investing is hard, it is intimidating, it is reserved for those with copious wealth, and it will cost you before it can offer dividends—and responded with a defiant smackdown that rendered all of that increasingly less true.

First Out of the Gate Will Stumble

The Robinhood journey has not been without hiccups. The app has suffered outages that were significant enough (one whole day here, a few hours there) to cause all of those who heralded its sudden success to declare the death of Robinhood with equal speed and glee. But even in wildly turbulent financial times, Robinhood has raised funds and is growing.

Robinhood persevered by looking at the specifics of engagement, focusing in on how one share of stock is an investment that is worthy of the trade and how that trade should be available to anyone interested in engaging in the conversation. Leveling the financial playing field was at the heart of every decision made and every service offered, and the cultural shift it has inspired will be felt for years to come.

Even some of the most innovative, creative, and driven entrepreneurs understand that it's impossible to pursue every opportunity. As Apple cofounder Steve Jobs said at a Worldwide Developers Conference in 1997, "People think focus means saying yes to the thing you've got to focus on. But that's not what it means at all. It means saying no to the hundred other good ideas that there are. You have to pick carefully. I'm actually as proud of the things we haven't done as the things I have done. Innovation is saying no to one thousand things."[14]

As your company grows, you'll be faced with all kinds of opportunities. The bigger you get, the more choices you'll face. It's exciting. It's challenging. It holds incredible promise. But it can be deadly. If you pursue too many different courses, you'll lose your focus, you'll find it difficult to execute your business strategy, you'll burn out your people, and you'll burn through your cash. When you focus in and execute better than anyone else can, you can offer an experience that improves someone's ability to do, play, and participate in ways they couldn't before.

Lens 2

CUSTOMIZE AND MAKE IT PERSONAL

Distinct from zooming in, customizing is the lens that guides you to think about how you can take what you do and know best and make it specific to the region, type, or personality of your customers. Properly executed, customizing takes the best of both segmentation (intending your product for an identifiable group of customers—say, people with curly hair) and personalization (allowing the customer to provide enough personal information to help you create a product that speaks to them as an individual) to produce a differentiation that results in loyalty by providing precisely the right thing at the right time.

The concept of customizing is not a new one, of course. But with so much of it coming on the heels of recent technological advancement, it's easy to forget that the idea of knowing your customer, identifying what they want and what they like, and delivering to them something they could make themselves has been around for some time. In a conversation with me, Bob Pittman, cofounder of MTV and current chairman and CEO of iHeartMedia, reminisced about the role radio played, and still plays for some, in what music people know about. In the days of yore, Casey Kasem would deliver his Top 40 every Sunday, and those songs would be the soundtrack of that week in much of the United States. Today, we have access to so much more music because of streaming services like Spotify, but that increased access can make it difficult to find your way to something new that you'll like. "On Spotify, most of the usage is not people picking their own songs. It's not people making their own playlist. It's people listening to somebody else's playlist because that someone else has done all the work. And, to some extent, that's what a radio station is: 'I trust Z100. They play music I like.'"[1]

There are loads of ways a company can take the boon that is a wealth of choice and respond to the fact that too much choice leads to an inability to enjoy anything. Spotify offers premade and shared playlists. Many large retail clothing stores offer a personal shopper. "It goes back to your time thing, in a time-crunch world with so many people screaming at you online and offline," Pittman said. "If marketers could cut *that* noise out? They can win. It's always about making it easy for me, making it simple. Curate my life for me? Yes, please—what would I give?"[2]

A TAILOR TAILORS TO CUSTOMERS

When you picture customization or tailoring, you need look no further than tailoring itself. I had long bought my dress shirts from known brands in department stores (entities about which you will now only learn in history classes). For a long time, the idea of having a bespoke shirt—one made to my specific measurements—was reserved for those willing to shell out far more than I was. Back then, buying custom shirts meant paying premium prices for what could only be provided with bespoke hand stitching. But with the advent of technology that made measurement-taking far easier, while still providing the indulgent fit, that premium price lowered to that of a high-end dress shirt. At one point, I learned of a Hong Kong tailor who made regular visits to the United States for fittings and then provided shirts that were made for me, and only me, at a price competitive with those of the high-end shirts I'd been buying. The move ruined me for the off-the-rack options that did not hug my shoulders and offer me the perfect neck opening. Even better, once my measurements were on file, I had only to remain the same general size (or wait until another round of measurements could be taken), and I could have as many shirts as I needed. My loyalty was predicated on a combination of the first taste of a perfect fit, a competitive price, and an ease of use, especially once my measurements had been taken. This is tailoring in every sense—more available and inspiring loyalty in a satisfied customer.

Price pressure from discounters, market disruption from online players, and shoppers with access to price transparency are but a few of the challenges facing we who are looking to identify, capture, and retain customers. Creating shareable video advertising, running Super Bowl ads, and creating promotional bells and whistles will only go so far; these strategies are easily and quickly replicated by competitors known and new. When you tailor things to your customers better than your competitors do, it is the difficulty with which they can replicate it that will determine your success.

Meeting customers' expectations for a personalized experience means learning from those who came before, availing yourself of advances made in technology, and applying those to the expertise you bring to your marketplace.

Some consumers demand this level of attention. Thanks to online pioneers such as Amazon, customers have grown to expect and desire personalized experiences. A survey of one thousand US adults by Epsilon and GBH Insights found that most respondents (80 percent) want personalization from retailers.[3] Amazon learned that it could sell more and offer true time savings (and a few cents off, to boot) by having subscription services for everyday products that are ordered with some regularity. The customer gains the service of not running out of what they use regularly, and Amazon provides the ability to establish what customers want and how often they want it, with the ability to turn off the automatic subscription as they wish. As Jenna Levin, sales manager at Amazon, explained to me, the execution Amazon offers required the company to think through all the various ways a person might want to use a subscription as well as think through consumer behavior so the user interface reflects the natural rhythms of providing what they want and how much they want it.

CUSTOMIZATION, PERSONALIZATION, AND SCIENCE

Paco Underhill is an environmental psychologist, an author, and the founder of market-research and consulting company Envirosell. He offers an understanding of human behavior that is based on the idea that where we are (the physical place) dictates a significant portion of our behavior. He takes this idea and applies it to figuring out what kind of environment makes for the most retail activity. He spoke to me about how tailoring your product is about seeing opportunities to take what you do well and figuring out how to recreate it in such a way that conforms to the specifics of your customers' lives and experiences. In the case of a laundry-detergent company, for example, he proposed offering the option of bespoke detergent. A detailed questionnaire would be furnished, and what you own (a lot of linen, more cotton than rayon, a preponderance of wool socks, workout clothing, etc.), the quality of your water (is it hard? Soft?), and the kind of washing machine you have would all be taken into consideration—and a laundry detergent (or detergents) would be custom blended according to your household's needs. It would do a better job cleaning your clothes, and you'd feel wedded to a product toward which you'd feel a proprietary kinship that would've been difficult to inspire had it not been personalized in some way.[4]

What are customers expecting? From the start of their interactions with their retailer of choice, they want to feel served in a way that recognizes who they are as individuals, with multiple touchpoints that enable them to allocate their time and money according to preferences they, as consumers, are increasingly aware of. In the best personalized experiences, retailers make the customer part of the dialogue and make use of data to create one-to-one personalization. Customers find retailers where they are naturally inclined to be (physically and online) and receive offers and packages targeted to them as individuals, with products, offers, and communications that are uniquely relevant to them.[5]

Netflix Rolls with the Times

The story of Netflix is one of customization. As Katie Ryan, group planning director at BBDO, framed it for me, what started as a mail-order system by which you could rent and return your movies and other DVDs then led the move to streaming based on what customers *didn't* want. "When Netflix started," she explained, "it was basically a repository of all content that no one wanted to watch. Today, it's an absolutely different experience. Now it's the home of serialized television that threw out the window the original, network-produced, twenty-four-episode-season concept that previously dominated that world."[6] Netflix saw what its customers didn't want and positioned itself to provide them with something distinctly different.

Netflix started in response to Blockbuster; it figured out how to get you your specific DVD for your planned weekend viewing, relieving you of being dependent on what happened to be available at the video-rental store. And Netflix figured out how to do so with the least burden to your busy schedule. It moved us all into the world of streaming and rendered us all viewers who watch what we want, when we want—all of it just a click away. As Ryan points out, the offerings weren't always great. So eventually, Netflix became a programmer of both the acquired and the original. It created a system by which it knew what to offer and how to make the user interface simple enough for any kind of adopter—old or young—to use it with relative ease, and it turned its eye to keeping up with the times.

With flexibility and tailoring and by moving with the times, Netflix introduced content, even some original content, on its streaming platform while still allowing users to continue to use DVD services so that the company could cover all of the bases of this particular market. If you wanted to view something at home and preferred or could only view that movie on DVD, Netflix had it; if you preferred to stream it and it was available in that form, Netflix offered that as well.

When the time came to shutter the DVD service, the streaming end of things was exploding. In fact, Netflix was the first to recognize that some people needed to be able to download their content (for flights or other spaces in which connectivity would be limited or absent) and tailored its product accordingly. Because Netflix knew so much about what its customers were viewing, it had the demographic information to start creating content themselves, content based on what it already knew about its users. Today, Netflix continues to identify the next step in the consumer-experience evolution. Where once the average viewer expected and looked for serialized content that would last eighteen, twenty, or twenty-four episodes in a given season with multiple (four, six, maybe even ten) seasons total, Netflix saw the attention span of its viewers dwindling. It customized the viewing experience to one where it told a story in six to eight episodes in a single, one-off season, which hit the mark perfectly. This allowed viewers to build deeper relationships with characters without needing to make the longer time commitment required by the network season. Each step Netflix made was tailored to the way consumers' behavior changed, and it participated in changing that behavior, too.

Distinguishing yourself in the marketplace comes in the form of creating unique experiences that are tailored and speak directly to customers as individuals.

Configuration Is Personal

Dell was an early adopter of customization. When Michael Dell started the company in 1984, he did so with the belief that by selling personal-computer systems directly to consumers—not through big-box, general tech stores—Dell could better understand customers' needs and tailor products with the most effective computing solutions to meet those needs. Rather than going to a store and buying a computer with preestablished configurations deemed "best" for "most" people, you could call Dell directly and have one tailored to your needs. You called the shots in regard to the speed of your processor, the storage level—the options of any kind.

Insurance Isn't One-Size-Fits-All

Coming from the mathematical side of the customization coin is Progressive and its "gamification" approach to tailoring car insurance. As explained to me by Oded Koenigsberg, professor of marketing at London Business School and coauthor of *The Ends Game*, Progressive took the approach that "no two drivers are the same . . . why should their insurance be?"[7] In exchange for sharing driving data, a person can get a personalized quote. What was once a limited set of metrics—proxies of driving ability and risk pooling—became an almost fun interactive approach a person could use in order for their insurance to reflect their actual on-the-road behavior.

This was accomplished through something called Snapshot, a pay-per-use insurance program Progressive launched in 2008 to collect "information about how you drive, how much you drive, and when you drive."[8] Using a smartphone app or device that plugs directly into a vehicle, it records basic info (when you drive and for how long, and noting abrupt changes in speed, which are defined by hard brakes or quick accelerations). The smartphone app will also note the use of that device while in the vehicle. At the end of a trial period, a quote is issued and the vast majority of those who complete the trial see a reduction in premiums. Of course, a vast majority is not *all* users, which means there are those who use Snapshot for whom premiums either remain the same or see some increase. It also goes without saying that safe drivers are a self-selecting population, so the outcome of these trials does not speak to an issue of across-the-board excessive premiums.

What's interesting about this particular form of tailoring to a specific customer is the extent to which it makes evident a truth that is far from surprising: companies offer value to customers when customers give something back in exchange for that value. In the case of Progressive, it's information. To get the discount and keep it, the information has to keep coming. That information will shift and the meaning of that information will grow as the pool of data includes more people. The ability to prove that one is, in fact, a "good driver" is an enormous lure; to be able to save money because you have proven what you've long claimed is the type of satisfaction that will keep customers coming back for more while remaining willing to keep information flowing into the coffers.[9]

The Hardware and Software Question

Former Facebook CMO Gary Briggs framed the whole topic of tailoring and customization in today's market with a fascinating paradigm. Much of the business world can be broken down into one of hardware and software.

"And a lot more businesses are software businesses than there appear to be," he said. "For example, one of the reasons that Tesla is doing so well is a software point rather than just a hardware point."[10] Tesla produces a car, yes, but unlike most cars, the vast majority of what the Tesla does is modifiable. This ability to customize and adapt allows something that is fixed for most (BMW, Toyota, etc.) to be open to tailoring with the technology that makes Tesla Tesla. "It's gotten Tesla a lot of notoriety. It's what it means to own a vehicle that has a lot more to do with software than hardware."[11] How extraordinary is it if you can get into one car on Tuesday and get into a different one the following Monday? And you need not even wait until Monday because the updates can happen overnight. Once that becomes the norm, where do you go from there? Briggs described this whole new generation of people for whom the benefits of technology are a given—the ability to transform, do an update, fix the problem, identify the weakness, and insert a defense after the fact—a generation that doesn't always realize just how transformative this technology is or how recently this capacity emerged. "It's hard sometimes to get perspective when you've always been in it," he said.[12] This makes the challenge of knowing where next to go—what next to transform—what differentiates the company that stays ahead of the curve from the one that doesn't.

An emphasis on software makes tailoring possible; to tailor effectively and to the kind of extraordinary lengths that make for shareable, extraordinary experiences, an organization needs to embrace flexibility as a defining characteristic.

WeWork Is Where and If You Want to Be There

WeWork is one of those companies that took a seemingly hardware-based industry (office space is a rather concrete entity) and made it a software offering (by finding new and different ways to build flexibility into people's relationship to that real estate). It read the tea leaves well, then faded and flopped (somewhat)—because of overspending and the classic case of an entrepreneur who started with a big idea, built to scale, but couldn't manage the business when it scaled—and then rose again in the face of the landscape that continued to shift. Initially, WeWork was about how to offer offices to those who can't or won't commit to a space and want to expand horizons for themselves or their group by exploring different spaces, cities, or even countries in the pursuit of workspaces that make great work possible. So when the whole go-to-the-office thing became a concept of the past with the onset of the COVID-19 pandemic, WeWork's mission was thought to be dead and, with it, the entity that dominated its execution.

From the start, it wasn't completely clear what WeWork was or intended to be. It had a tech feel to it, yet it aimed its sights on real estate. As more and more property got scooped up, the lines blurred furiously. By the time the company's valuation had plummeted and its IPO plans had gone *poof*, many looked away in disinterest. WeWork went public via a SPAC at a $10 billion valuation, down significantly from the $47 billion it was valued at after raising $1 billion in its SoftBank-led Series H round in January 2019. Cofounder and then-CEO Adam Neumann stepped down later that year amid allegations of poor management, arrogance, and potential illegal activity. WeWork has since been trying to redeem itself and turn around investor—and public—perception. Chairman Marcelo Claure initiated a strategic five-year turnaround plan in February 2020,[13] naming a real-estate, not tech, executive as its new CEO.

As WeWork embraced flexibility, the first things to go were the long-term leases and members-only approach it previously had. New "On Demand" and "All Access" options allowed people who, amid pandemic-necessitated work from home and remote schooling, needed to get out of their homes to go, even once a week, to spaces that offered a different view that did not include their teenage son drumming his fingers incessantly while ignoring his history class on screen. WeWork also offered opportunities of a kind previously unconsidered; for example, to universities that needed more space for their students to study as they looked for on-campus life that still allowed for more social distancing. As Prabhdeep Singh, WeWork's global head of marketplace, explained,

> What we've essentially done is unbundle our space. It used to be that the only way to enjoy our spaces was via a bundled subscription product and monthly memberships. But we realized with COVID, the world was shifting, and [we needed] to open up our platform to a broader group of people and make it as flexible as humanly possible. So they can now book a room for a half hour or get a day pass, for example. The use cases are so wide. Over the last year and a half, we've been really figuring out what things we want to focus on and what things we don't. As a flexible space provider, we are looking at where the world is going.[14]

As I said, flexibility is at the core of effective tailoring that will appeal to customers now and have the best chance of remaining a player down the line. WeWork became the answer for the merry band of nomads so many of us have become. When your team lives in five different states and two time zones, you have occasion to need space in different places for some or a lot of the time. WeWork offers that. And when a group without a home base seeks a way to kick into creative high gear or generate a bit of teamwork mojo, WeWork offers something for them, too. And WeWork does so in a way that is fit for that particular group, that person, that idea, that situation—because it can. It can become whatever someone needs it to be.

Hotel Life Made Your Way

Dr. Samantha Sterling, chief strategy officer at ad agency AKQA across Asia-Pacific, talked to me about a customization program they tried at a leading hotel chain in Australia. The goal: for guests to feel able to have a personalized experience while staying at one of their hotels.

She told me about one of their more successful experiments, in which

the basic premise was to use the emails you receive before you check into a hotel [that] say, "Hey, you know, get ready for your stay tomorrow. Tell us what time [you'll] arrive," and all that sort of stuff. We added a URL to the bottom of that email and said, "Click here to personalize your room." On that page, you could choose the temperature of the room, choose a pillow type or density, and choose the contents of your minibar from one of these packs. For the mini fridge, you could pick a package: a budget-conscious version, a health-conscious option, and a luxury option. All of it was available in the convenience store downstairs, but the point was to bring it bedside.[15]

This is a terrific example of making use of preexisting tools: a low-tech questionnaire, food and drink options already in the hotel, bedding also already present and accounted for, and a thermostat that just needed to be set at a temperature. They figured out a way to hand all of this control to the customer—letting them design their experience and making them feel heard and served—all while the hotel did what it was going to do anyway. The mini fridge needs to be filled with something. The beds all have pillows. The thermostat will be on.

Are there ways your organization can use what you already do and have to put the customer in the driver's seat? Control is personalization. The power to personalize makes customers feel like they're in an open conversation with their supplier, and that's what will result in loyalty and habitual returns.

A CLOSER LOOK: PERSONAL SHOPPING AND STYLE DELIVERED TO YOUR DOOR: STITCH FIX

Some of the most impressive examples of personalization come from brands that turn it into an entire business model, delivering 100-percent personalized experiences for every customer.

Clothing retailer Stitch Fix, founded in 2011 by Katrina Lake and former J. Crew buyer Erin Morrison Flynn, has the goal of making the shopping experience personal. At the heart of the business is the idea that a stylist who has taken the time to listen to what you already know about what you like, what you believe looks good on yourself, and the occasions for which you tend to dress can make suggestions that fit your usual style as well as stretch your usual preferences to invite some new ideas. A questionnaire, access to social-media accounts, and a description of yourself in some detail allows a stylist to home in on and provide several options so that the busy, hates-to-shop person can have their wardrobe revitalized on a regular basis. As the company learns about your taste, the recommendations become more suited to you, which means more purchases and more revenue. In each box of clothing and accessories, a customer receives five options. The customer chooses how often they want to receive their options (every two weeks, once a month, once every two months) and, once they receive them, has three days to choose to keep some, all, or none of the items offered. If they keep at least one item, the styling fee is credited toward the purchase of that item; if they keep everything, they get 25 percent off the whole shipment. Stitch Fix uses data science, machine learning (AI), and human stylists to create its style options.[16]

The startup isn't merely selling clothes; it's selling personalized style recommendations—entire wardrobes curated for each customer based on their personal preferences, size, and feedback. The very name—Stitch (clothing) and Fix (addressing a problem)—speaks to its bold intent. The monthly structure makes it feel like a gift, one you give yourself, that allows you to have a treat, something new to add to your wardrobe, and puts a little spring in your step on a regular basis—all with no effort once you've provided the company with the data it needs to know what to send.

Let me be clear: I am the very definition of someone who is miles away from the target audience for Stitch Fix. But even from way over here, I can see the beauty, the purpose, and the elegance of the execution in Lake's enterprise. She, like me, found shopping exhausting. Choice does not produce pleasure. Quite the opposite—faced with racks of clothing in stores, I end up in a dressing room with the pants I've somewhat randomly grabbed off the rack, miserable and surrounded by more failures than success. If I'm lucky, some salesperson takes enough pity on me to contribute to my experience, but depending on their eye, taste, and knowledge of inventory, this accomplishes only so much. Online, the choices are even greater, and my eyes glaze over with greater speed. What Lake has done, for the pro shopper and shopping-averse alike, is take the best features of a great personal shopper—tailoring and customizing choices—and delivering those options to your door.

The beauty of her concept is in the way the company makes use of information, learning about you as a customer, at a time when stores offer less and less service. Stitch Fix takes the idea of a stylist and adds a dollop of data science to brew the perfect concoction that is clothing you are likely to both like and fit into. As someone who has little to no preference about what I wear, I still find it interesting to hear Lake talk about how, as brick-and-mortar retail reduced its presence and the online world grew, consumers lost the human touch in ways that were deeply felt. That thing that used to happen in small, independent shops—where, when you walked in, the owner would say, "So glad you're here. I just got in some sweaters that will look great on you and have that collar you love in the cotton weight you prefer"—is no more. As that world of owners and sales reps who know you began to be replaced by mass efficiency, where selection is greater but support in making your way through it is sparse, Lake took the realm of clothing and tried to wrangle it into a place where you could get the personal attention and service of the past as well as today's abundance of selection.

It is not unrelated that Lake came from a venture-capital firm. She understood well that it is not enough to have a good idea; success is found in the execution. And she chose an industry where the execution was going to be incredibly difficult. The range of sizes, colors, and other options for any given piece of clothing, not to mention the challenges of sourcing the inventory and understanding how best to gather and use data for styling purposes, builds in a level of complexity that would bring down the faint of heart, not to mention doing it at scale. Whereas a small shop, carrying a finite number of items in an even smaller number of iterations, with a customer base limited to the local environs, has one task, Lake's was infinitely more complex.

Lake needed the service she provided to stand up to and even exceed the expectations of what is a demanding clientele. Busy customers with careers and families want an interface that will save them time and provide an outcome that used to depend on significant time being spent. Lake's insight was to invite her customers to expect to be delighted by a once-a-month package that would contain clothing that they would like, was likely to fit, reflected current fashion, and came in at the budget they predetermined. Even from my sartorially challenged place in the world, I could see how this would be an enormous boon to anyone who loves clothes, cares about being au courant, and wants the best without having to go out and look for it.

Users provide relevant data about themselves, and Stitch Fix analyzes that data against the clothing patterns of consumers with similar tastes.

This way, the data and fundamental preferences of the user base are built into the options available to the humans who step in and work with the data. As Lake explained in a piece she wrote for the *Harvard Business Review*,

> Data science isn't woven into our culture; it *is* our culture. We started with it at the heart of the business, rather than adding it to a traditional organizational structure, and built the company's algorithms around our clients and their needs. We employ more than eighty data scientists, the majority of whom have PhDs in quantitative fields such as math, neuroscience, statistics, and astrophysics. Data science reports directly to me, and Stitch Fix wouldn't exist without data science. It's that simple.[17]

Stitch Fix delivers a truly personalized customer experience from the very first interaction, and the service only improves as it learns more about individual users.

A CLOSER LOOK: GIFTING EXPERIENCE, FUN, AND DIFFERENCE: ZOLA

I've been invited to and attended a lot of weddings over the last several decades, and I've had one myself. Like all guests, I've been faced with the gift-buying moment when you scan the registry and wonder how to choose a meaningful gift. That is, how to pick a gift that is something the newly married duo actually wants and can use—and that might remind them of the friend they have in me. Invariably, the registry is where creative gift giving goes to die. No fun, no whimsy, and almost never a space in which I or anyone else can offer more than a *thing*.

One year, a couple I knew was getting married at their house near a lake—and I wanted to give them something that they'd remember was from me, not just another place setting for their flatware. With this in mind, I got together with some friends, and we bought the newly married couple a canoe. This was no small project. I gathered interested parties together and figured out which canoe we wanted to give, and then the really hard part began. Have you ever tried to buy a canoe and have said canoe delivered? It's not easy.

For my own wedding, my wife controlled the registry, and we ended up with a lot of lovely household items. But I wanted a TV for our kitchen, and since the registry was done through typical bridal places, like Bloomingdale's and Bed Bath & Beyond, where not many TVs are sold, our registry did not include it. When we received a TV for the kitchen, it was only because a friend knew of my wish and went off menu.

Now, I go to a lot of weddings—of the children of my friends—and the song has stayed largely the same. The registries look eerily similar, and there are few, if any, opportunities to give something that is a reflection of my relationship to the couple or my wish to start them off in a creative and interesting way. So when I learned of Zola, I was immediately intrigued.

The founders of Zola faced the same problem I did and decided to create registries that allowed for more creativity—that allowed *experiences* to be gifted. This made for some interesting challenges in terms of infrastructure. To start: inventory, and how to avoid it entirely while still managing the customer experience in a way that reflects well on the Zola brand. Linking to a partner or other retailer would run the risk of sending customers further on, and the chances that customers could have for a bad experience that Zola wouldn't be able to control (yet for which they would be blamed) would increase tenfold. So they landed on a registry that was a true combination of an e-commerce or retail business one combined with a drop-ship model where Zola doesn't take the inventory, but it does ship the products purchased directly from brands to the home. Cofounder Shan-Lyn Ma's background at Gilt and in retail sales meant she understood which questions to ask, what operations were needed, and what the customer experience she wanted to create would look like from every side. She spoke with as many people as she could in order to understand the experience of those she wanted her idea to target.

Those getting married today are looking to own less and experience more. Zola allows you to fund a honeymoon trip or, say, buy a canoe. The ability to contribute to a gift that has meaning rather than choosing the cheapest item off a registry ("Look! There's the spoon I got you!") was a big part of the inspiration for Zola. When Ma was thinking about the dilemma from the point of view of the gift giver, she mentioned her idea to someone who had recently gotten married. He talked about the challenges he and his spouse had faced getting married. This friend and his now-wife had huge fights about their registry, making yet another aspect of the wedding process fraught.

Why had it been so difficult? Because the registry process was stuck in the 1960s. People who had never stepped foot in places like Bloomingdale's or Neiman Marcus were suddenly locked into accessorizing their lives from those places. The people you knew best, the people you wanted to join you on your important and special day, weren't able to give you a gift that reflected that intimacy. It made no sense.

Zola allows a couple to ask for what they actually want, such as contributions toward a down payment for a home or an IVF treatment, and makes it possible for multiple guests to pitch in to buy larger-ticket items and/or things the couple wouldn't have thought of. Ma wanted to create thoughtful options for people like herself—people who'd faced a registry on which they could afford only a single teaspoon. (When she asked the bride about it, she admitted to a limited registry because she couldn't deal with coordinating with multiple stores.) Ma wanted to provide alternative ways to express love toward new couples.

Faced with a challenge that has as much to do with the experience of the user as it does with the recipient, Zola stands as a stunning example of a well-defined problem being addressed through experience alone.

Examining your industry or organization for ways to tailor or customize what you do to the customer you want to bring in or retain requires two important things: knowledge of what you offer and a deep understanding of who your consumer can be. Tailoring includes offering product choices (e.g., Blue Apron allows you to craft your family's weekly menu to suit the newly vegetarian teen in your house) and regional distinctions (e.g., the Barnes & Noble in El Paso will offer different selections than those of the store in the Upper West Side of Manhattan). Customization acknowledges specifics, within a broad category, as in the case of the laundry detergent Paco Underhill discussed, formulated based on the responses to a survey about the type of wardrobe and linens found in a given home.

In other words, "listen first, act second." When you want to change how people do things, you need to start with seeing the opportunity first. Then, you must listen to your customer, understand how they're thinking, become part of the fabric of their lives, and strive to understand who they know themselves to be. Once I put my name on my first baseball glove, broke it in using hot oil, and caught my first line drive with it, I never looked at another glove again. It became my glove. This is the way you tailor and customize an experience that will change a customer's behavior and routine. If you customize your product or experience, you build a crazy glue–type relationship between you and your customer.

Lens 3

JOINING FORCES

Joining forces is about building your audience exponentially to solve a bigger problem than what you alone can best address, creating an entirely new experience from the forces of two discrete organizations. Joining forces is not about branding. It is not about simply improving the service you already provide. This isn't just getting Michael Jordan to sign a run of sneakers; that's just the same product with a premium value attached.

Some partnerships make obvious sense. Starbucks plays music in its buildings; partnering with Spotify to promote artists and the music-streaming platform for the customers both organizations were already sharing only solidified and grew audiences for the two powerhouses. It created a new experience in which music discovery and sharing became an implicit part of sitting and enjoying a half-caf skinny latte with a caramel drizzle.

What about your business? Is there some aspect over which you command a level of understanding and quality of service that you might bring to another company in the name of improving your customers' experience, expanding the number of people able to consume what you do and creating an entirely new experience from the merging of ideas?

In today's world, some of the most important marketing tools are not those you pay for or place, or for which you decide the parameters. Instead, some of the most effective marketing is found in the words and images of social media where, as it is generally understood, no one shares the ordinary. Rather, we share, recommend, and create momentum toward that which is extraordinary. What can your company do to create an experience that is shareable? Where is the opportunity for your organization to join forces to create the extraordinary?

CATCH ME IF YOU CAN COMES TO JFK

No one shares the ordinary. "Average is over," as Tom Friedman told me when I interviewed him for my previous book, *Shift Ahead*.[1] In a world where people only share what's extraordinary, creating experiences that meet that threshold often means joining forces between two already-strong market presences.

The TWA Hotel at John F. Kennedy International Airport is a hotel that defies all the usual expectations for an airport hotel. Typically, an airport hotel is a place that could be anywhere and therefore is precisely the same across all cities and states. Close your eyes and picture the lobby, the elevator, the hall, the room—you could be imagining any airport hotel in any airport, anywhere. But Trans World Airlines (an airline founded by Howard Hughes that, with Pan Am, made flying, as Diane Keaton said in *Annie Hall*, "la-di-da") Hotel is a deliberately nostalgic romp. From the pool to the lounges, to the invitation to roller-skate to your terminal, to the rooms that speak to glamour from a different time, it seeks to stand apart and change your experience of what it means to stay at an airport hotel.

The TWA Hotel experience strives to take you out of the routinized zombie-walk that flying has become. Once upon a time, people dressed up to fly. People experienced the opportunity to get from Point A to Point B with such speed and precision as something to revel in. In return, the airlines made you feel like a guest, like someone worth taking the time to treat well and for whom they wanted to create an experience. Today, we all know this is not the case, no matter how many times they thank you for choosing them for your flying needs, no matter how many times they invite you to tell them what they can do for you.

But the TWA Hotel says, "Let us take you to a different time and place. Let us make you feel like someone worth dressing up for. Let us make this fun and give you plenty of reasons to share the moments you experience. Let us take all the basic facets of a hotel stay—the room, entertainment spaces, and food—and raise the bar significantly." The hotel does this by availing itself of the low expectations that come with the words "JFK" and "hotel" and turning them on their ear. They do so by taking the spirit of *Catch Me If You Can*, with Leonardo DiCaprio racing through halls of the airport, and bringing you to all the nostalgic glamour suggested therein. Bottom line: If you're going to stay at an airport, why would you dare stay at a Marriott Courtyard? Why not stay at a place that's going to allow you to get on your social media and say, "Look at me and my fun, fabulous life," even when doing something as mundane as spending the night at the airport?

TO SLEEP IN VAN GOGH'S BED

The Art Institute of Chicago offered a similar experience in 2016 when it commissioned a re-creation of Vincent van Gogh's famous bedroom and made it available to rent on Airbnb for just $10 a night in Chicago's River North neighborhood. They designed the room according to van Gogh's *Bedroom in Arles* paintings and made it so specifically to order that the listing had to specify that the bed was not built for tall people and that, while two people could technically rent the room, only those inclined toward close proximity would be comfortable, as the room was built for one. Their eye for detail took precedence over any and all tendencies toward pampering: the colors of the walls, the structure of the furniture—even the bowl and pitcher were present and accounted for. The listing was created as part of an exhibition at the Institute called "Van Gogh's Bedrooms," which brought together the three paintings of the same name that van Gogh created while living in the "Yellow House" in Arles, France. Even the price of the listing reflected the poverty-stricken conditions of van Gogh's life.

The experience that Airbnb and the Art Institute of Chicago created by joining forces stands out in so many ways. They identified the ways in which participants could do something that was eminently shareable, something unlikely to be done anywhere else, and, more importantly, that flew in the face of the common approach most experiences entailed—to appeal to as many people as possible. The $10 rental price, short bed, and sparsely appointed space with no fancy bathroom shower were, quite explicitly, not for everyone. They narrowed their focus on a particular type of user and made an experience to thrill them that each organization alone could not have pulled off. It was a huge idea that could not have emerged from any one mind or entity. And the social-media attention garnered at the time was extraordinary and entirely earned.

A CLOSER LOOK: TO SLEEP, PERCHANCE TO DREAM: CASPER

Our bedtime story begins with four entrepreneurs who were looking for a category to disrupt during a time when there were plenty of investors and incubators in search of ideas to fund. The idea people in this scenario fit the bill perfectly. They were young and ambitious with bright, fresh eyes, looking for a business to start. As is so often the case, the market that eventually captured their imagination was one for which they had personal need: that of the mattress, that item we all need in one form or another, that thing that can be one of the biggest expenditures in a home, be it a first apartment or a palatial McMansion. Mattresses are notorious for the impervious fog that surrounds choosing the right one—how do you distinguish quality, where do you find the greatest options, and how can you do all of this when the media has made it clear that the industry itself is predicated on a lack of transparency with regard to pricing?

The founders of Casper brought some experience in direct marketing to the challenge and, like all of us, knew well how unpleasant the typical mattress-distribution options were and how fast-talking salespeople plus an inability to compare prices for the same product made the industry a necessary evil begging to be improved and disrupted.

In other words, the mattress industry is one that is musty, dusty, unpleasant, and understood to be one where a lack of transparency and ability to price shop leads to annoyance, disappointment, and a logistical nightmare. For younger generations, this meant doing anything to avoid buying a traditional mattress. Heading to a sleazy mattress store (no) or the department store their parents turned to (Macy's? Really?) was simply not going to happen. How, then, to sell to those who were not going to go where your product is sold? Even if you do figure out how to sell to those people, how do you get your mattress in front of people who don't shop at traditional mattress-selling outlets?

Casper managed to take a regular, non-innerspring mattress and compress it into an air-sealed bag, rolled tight for shipping. The shipping box is the size of a mini-fridge (a considerable reduction) and rendered a previously cumbersome item into one that could be handled by any of the available shipping means. But, given that this was a requisite for online purchases, Casper could not rest on this particular laurel. Mattresses were not yet ready for double-click buying without some tactile interaction. Consumers, even younger ones, were still constrained by a desire to interact physically with products (as we will discuss with the Getting Virtual lens). Mattresses, to the extent that people thought of buying them, landed firmly (pun very much intended) on the list of products that people wanted to feel and see for themselves.

So Casper needed a way to take the leap off the screen and into the world of bricks and mortar. But this needed to happen in a way that did not look like the old-school way, a way that would avail itself of the mechanical ingenuity that was its mattress in a box and allow the company to get the spotlight it so richly deserved. Casper needed a way to get what it was selling under its customers—literally.

No matter the customer, buying a mattress requires a big chunk of change, and most people go into the purchase believing only their back, legs, and head can discern whether or not a mattress is going to work for them. Casper knew better than to try building its own retail experience. Knowing when to stay in your lane to focus on doing what you do well is Lens 1 for a reason. What Lens 3, Joining Forces, speaks to is how to take what you do so well and work with someone else who does what they do well to make both of you better for it.

So Casper initially partnered with West Elm.

Why did this make so much sense? When you think about who is going to avoid the mattress store and the department store and be inclined to accept a narrow range of options in the name of brand recognition and ease of access, you think about millennials. They didn't want to go where their parents went, and West Elm was a brand that already drew them in. In Guy Raz's interview with Casper cofounder and former CEO Philip Krim, Krim talked about how West Elm allowed Casper's mattress to be seen as the finishing touch to a bedroom.[2] There are several theories as to why this was ultimately not the long-term solution to Casper's distribution challenges, but the initial thinking behind the partnership was extremely sound. They had the right customers and stores in the right neighborhoods, and the partnership allowed Casper to be a part of shareable experiences about which people who go to West Elm were inclined to post.

When the partnership crumbled, Casper came away having learned some key lessons about how to join forces in a way that will net the best results. Its timing for jumping on the West Elm wagon was not, perhaps, ideal. West Elm was at the other side of its peak, so it wasn't in a position to bolster the brand as it might have been able to do a few years earlier. In such a partnership, it is crucial for both sides to be solid in their own way, in their own industries, and in general. Taking this lesson forward, the next company with whom Casper joined forces, Target, felt like just the right next step. Target was interested in home "wellness," which included sleep. As Krim described to Raz, "Brian Cornell, the CEO of Target, said, 'The commercial opportunities are huge. I think we can build a big business together.'" With Target as a strategic investor and Casper mattresses on display in Target stores, a huge step forward took place, one that can be seen as a natural progression. Target has a hipster quality, is one of the few big-box stores with a decidedly millennial tilt (while still serving other generations with ease), and is ubiquitous in a way that West Elm wasn't.

Recognizing what it did well (make mattresses) and who it needed to reach (anyone who wants to sleep well—i.e., everyone), and having solved the question of how to sell a product in a way that didn't require a moving van (vacuum-sealed mattress, anyone?), Casper just needed to join forces with the right player (Target) to offer the experience it couldn't provide alone—the ability to touch its product.

And Casper did this without limiting future partnerships. Soon, Casper sprung up in Bed Bath & Beyond. American Airlines proudly touts its use of Casper's delightful wares for its first-class clients. Each partnership links "Casper" with "sleep." Casper, the sleep experts—and experts in identifying, working with, and getting their products to their customers by effectively joining forces with others.

LITERARY MULTITASKING FOR RUNNERS, WALKERS, AND LISTENERS OF ALL STRIPES: AUDIBLE

Don Katz, founder and creator of Audible, wrote the story of his company so well because he understood why someone would want a streaming service for audiobooks and other audio content to exist. He *was* that someone. As he has described, "I loved listening to well-composed, artfully performed words when I jogged in Riverside Park. I would listen in the old-school way, which was to have tapes in my belly pack. I always talked about the fact that they were profoundly inefficient. They froze in the winter. They would bake in the dashboard in the summer. There's nothing worse when you're aerobically taxed than trying to futz with them and change them out in your Walkman, an ancient device."[3]

As a writer—he was the technology columnist for *Esquire*—he covered some early media launches, like Time Warner's high-speed internet in Orlando, Florida, and interactive TV trials. He spent time with the people making the decisions that went into these launches and talked extensively with them about the strategic implications of the transitional state the world of media was in. Before that, as a young journalist, he had been based in London and covered war zones. In other words, the man had context. Context, detail, nuance—and he spent as much time thinking about ideas that failed (and why) as he did about those that succeeded (and why). By trade, he lived and breathed the details other people missed. And he wrote a book—described as "the best book on Sirius,"[4] according to Mitch Ratcliffe, the sustainability leader at Metaforce—called *The Big Store*. Ratcliffe described it as "very thoughtful about the implications of the technical, the digital transition, and how it's going to change the media business."[5] Katz's understanding of the universe into which he was about to wade was deep. He was forty-two, and he decided to throw everything he had into an entirely new venture.

It was the mid 1990s, and there was a lot going on. Format transitions of all kinds were in the air. If you had a VHS tape of a movie, you were considering buying it again on DVD. (And, a few years later, you would likely pay for it again when downloading it from Apple; quite the business model, right?) Foundational to Katz's idea for Audible was the concept that people were used to paying for continued access to the media they liked (Ratcliffe questions whether this tolerance exists anymore, but that's not the point here). What is relevant is that the idea of Audible came about at a time when there was a lot of physical transformation of platform in the air, with music going from tape to CD, videos going from VHS to DVD, and so on. Even without many of the channels and platforms that exist today, it was a time when things were moving away from traditional delivery systems, and the public was primed to accept these new formats.

Katz knew the experience he wanted: something that would allow him to multitask—specifically, to read books—while running. His mission was to develop the first downloadable audio player ever made, which is rather extraordinary in and of itself. And then there was the matter of what might play on that device. He used his knowledge of and relationship with the book-publishing world and his years of exposure and listening to insights from some of the biggest players in the tech and media worlds to create Audible.

Developing a device to play something in a format you are largely pioneering, the content of which has never been delivered in quite this way, was a big project. The level of expertise required for each of these elements was significant, and the person who thinks they can be all things to all people tends to drown in those elements. Katz told Raz about "trying to find anyone I could to talk about a future that involved these little devices that were filled with a sound, the soundscape of culture, basically the soundtrack of culture. And people thought I was out of my mind. So we wrote a business plan to create the company ourselves. And we called it Audible for audible words."[6]

It would have been understandable for the nascent organization to be focused on the hardware side of things, trying to make a player that lived up to what Katz imagined, rather than on the ephemeral heart of the enterprise: the book. And he did dive in, making what did not exist before. But he also got a lot of it wrong, and much of it was clumsy. His device had incredibly slow download speeds, and its software couldn't be updated. But he attended to all of the other aspects of business, too. Very soon, the skill with which he licensed and curated the content to go on that player became apparent.

The content was not without potential pitfalls and difficulties. He needed the big names, the top sellers, the kind of content people would take a chance on with a lesser-known method of delivery. He focused his energies on the big publishers, with an eye on the *New York Times* bestseller list and the most popular books from a given publisher. Remember, back then, there were a lot of publishers; all the consolidation we now see has happened in the last decade or so. Coordinating the top-selling books and negotiating the terms by which he might be able to offer them via this new medium took effort, an understanding of the kind of material that would translate best to the audio format, and an understanding of what the publishers would need in order to give him the rights to do so.

Katz hit all the right notes when it came to assembling the title list for Audible. Publishers became interested in doing more business with him, and customers started to prove themselves willing to listen to audiobooks in this form. At the time, as I discussed with Guy Raz, "There was no business. There were books on tape, but [Katz] really supercharged audiobooks in a way that I don't think anybody could have imagined. I know that with my book, we sold almost as many audiobooks as hardcovers. A huge number of people consume books now and talk about reading books by listening to them."[7] Katz tapped into an idea that led customers to where he knew they wanted to go—if only they knew—and he changed their behavior in a fundamental way. He did this with his idea, yes; it was an extraordinary vision. But it was propelled to the next level and was able to reach its audience because of an eventual joining of forces. Experiences changed and behavior was forever modified as a result of a union between Audible and Apple.

Audible's first download happened on October 31, 1997, at a tech conference. It was *Men Are from Mars, Women Are from Venus*, and the customer was in Arizona. Back then, the user interface involved an Audible website, and you would dock your device to the computer on which the website was loaded through a serial port. It took a long, long time to download a book. People typically left things downloading at night, used the device during the day, and redocked the device the next night.

Joining forces, the point of this lens, is when one entity takes its strength and joins it with the strength of another. Both sides of the transaction need to be at their fighting-weight best. And they need to understand not just the other side but also the enormous potential that comes with integrating what they do and how they do it with how another does what they do. And, of course, both sides need to want the merge and feel that the union is in some way meant to be or meaningfully opportune.

In 2003, Katz got called to the show. In this case, Steve Jobs wanted to talk to him about working together. You did not pitch Steve Jobs. You did not find ways to put yourself in his line of sight. If he wanted to see you, he did; if he didn't, there was not a lot you could do about it. Jobs liked what he saw in Audible. He called Katz and asked a lot of fairly detailed tech questions, and then they talked about audiobooks themselves. He wanted Katz to forget about his device and focus on what he did so well: curating content, making deals, and getting the most bang for his licensing bucks. Jobs told him about his next big thing: the iPod. And he told Katz he loved what he was doing. Katz recalls that Jobs told him how "he would weep copiously when he listened to E. B. White read *Charlotte's Web*."[8] He told Katz he was going to spend $15 million marketing the new-to-the-market iPod. He had a plan through which all of Katz's efforts would be heard by the world via the newly developing Apple iTunes Store—exclusively. According to Mitch Ratcliffe, "Steve said, 'Of all the things that I could want to hear, I love books more than I even love music.'"[9] Yes, there were other audiobook companies out there, but none had the list that Don Katz had cultivated at Audible. He had the books that Jobs wanted to listen to, the books Jobs wanted in his Apple store. So within three years, Audible was entirely out of the hardware business.

As Raz explained to me, "It's about somehow fundamentally under-standing that there is going to be a change, and like Steve Jobs said, cus-tomers don't know what they want; you have to lead them to it. And that's what Pat Brown is doing. That's what John Foley did. You know, that's what Don Katz did with Audible. Audible was almost bankrupt, you know—it almost went under in 2001. I think their stock price was at, like, forty cents or something."[10] Katz had an idea that could lead customers to what he knew they'd want, if only he could get them there. And he did it in his inimitable way. As Raz put it, "Everyone was looking forward, texting and digital, and [Katz] looked backwards at radio storytelling."[11]

In joining forces with Apple at the point of its iPod launch to offer its content exclusively, Audible made a deal that took all that was best about Audible and hitched it to a star that was Apple's iPod and its iTunes Store. Audible didn't just build on and make a deal with its own strength. Katz understood how to let his device go. He knew where his weakness was and didn't allow pride, or whatever else it is that can cause a company to cling to a proverbial sinking ship, to get in the way.

And Katz understood what, specifically, he had done so well. He understood where the market was when he was setting up his deals. Sure, he also had a sense of what the potential was down the line, but that wasn't going to be what the deal was about. This was a passion project on his part, and the market he was diving into was small. The publishers had already spent the money creating the audiobooks; the studio, the actors or authors, all of the costs had already happened. What Katz was offering was a way for them to get a bit more of it back. It was found money, and, in the grand scheme of things, none of the publishers expected, nor did they get, anything significant from the deals. By the time the audiobook market showed itself to be the moneymaker that it was, the deals were already done.

The beauty of this particular joining of forces is that it showed with absolute precision the importance of recognizing what isn't working and going into a deal with what you do best. It can be incredibly hard to build a product. It's hard at the inception, and, even worse, once you are in production—once you have that thing out in the world—it's hard to fix it when you realize you got something (or all of it) wrong.

Katz wanted to make the listening of books portable. He had a vision. He wanted to run with something other than music. Katz himself puts it best:

The story was that we would occupy this time of people's life, when your eyes are busy but your mind is free. We would create a higher level of purpose than the AM/FM radio. This wasn't for everyone; this was for *you*. You would be able to program your own listening time in the future, through digital technology. And we would have a company that would sell a solid-state digital device, as well as content. It would be about books and literature. It would allow you to listen in the fresh air and marketplace.[12]

By joining forces with Apple, he did just that.

A CLOSER LOOK: EXPLORE THE WORLD WITH THE ORIGINAL WORLD EXPLORERS: LINDBLAD EXPEDITIONS AND NATIONAL GEOGRAPHIC

Like many children in my generation, I used to eagerly await the arrival of the *National Geographic* magazine every month. With its book-like form and the distinctive yellow trim, *National Geographic* allowed me to explore the world I was learning about, from the solar system to the oceans, from wildlife to indigenous tribes in South America, and from historical topics to geography. I cherished those monthly moments of adventure in its pages and, like many Americans, had a pile of them in my room and, later on, piles of them in my basement. But as time marched on, and as I grew up, I stopped renewing the subscription. It never stopped being of interest to me, but it fell from my immediate imagination to something that I was content to enjoy on those days in the waiting room when my doctor ran late.

It never left my imagination, especially not the vivid, spectacular images of places and peoples I figured I'd never encounter in person. *National*

Geographic's photography is iconic. It allows you to be in the Serengeti, on the surface of Mars, deep in the ocean, or in Antarctica. It transports you, through the power of its photographers, to those exotic locations. Fast forward many, many years to when I was lucky enough to take my family on an adventure, the likes of which the young me could never have imagined: a National Geographic Lindblad Expedition, one that took us to Alaska. I was not a big cruise person, having been on only one or two before. But this wasn't just a cruise. It was an adventure that allowed me to bring my childhood love of vicarious *National Geographic* adventure and experience it in the real world, beyond the page.

When we went on the expedition, the experience did not disappoint. As we traveled through the Alaskan glaciers, the *National Geographic* naturalists explained what we were seeing in a way that felt deep, rich, and authentic. It was like I was in the magazine, traveling with a reporter, listening as they narrated what was interesting about the glaciers or the icebergs or the whales breaching in front of us. A *National Geographic* photographer worked with me to help me get the perfect picture of the whale as it breached. In the evenings, there were lectures by naturalists that took us through the history of the environment in Alaska, along with so many other topics. It was, to say the least, an extraordinary learning experience. By taking all that was uniquely appealing about *National Geographic* and combining it with the authentic and exciting adventure of the Lindblad Expeditions brand, they created an experience that was like transporting me into the pages of the magazine and allowed me to be an explorer just as I had imagined it many, many years ago, reading through *National Geographic*'s pages and looking at its stunning pictures.

As you might guess, once we returned home, mine were the vacation pictures friends voluntarily asked to see.

Lindblad Expeditions tours are known for opening up the world of wildlife and adventure, so when it joined forces with National Geographic, it was a match made in heaven. The consumers for both organizations shared so much in common but hadn't yet met one another.

For those who think of cruising as sitting by a pool with a cocktail and getting off the ship occasionally to shop the jewelry kiosks while being led through the pier-adjacent tourist traps, a Lindblad cruise is completely different. Regarded as the father of ecotourism, Lars-Eric Lindblad was the first travel-company owner to take travelers where only scientists had gone before. In other words, he was the first to have the insight that there are folks who want travel to be purposeful and genuinely transformative. As is so often the case, inspiration came in the form of wish fulfillment; Lindblad himself really wanted to be an explorer, and he eventually channeled his passion into creating a travel business that offered what he always wanted. A noted environmentalist, he was the first to bring those with an adventurous spirit to the most exotic places in the world, including Antarctica, Svalbard, the Galápagos Islands, Easter Island, the Amazon, Papua New Guinea, and Bhutan, all with the focus of creating experiences that would foster an understanding and appreciation for the planet.

In 1979, Lars-Eric's son, Sven-Olof Lindblad, took over the company and expanded the vision by adding newer and more immersive ecotourism experiences. Unfortunately, despite creating these incredible experiences, his remained a niche brand, one relatively unknown outside of those intrepid types specifically interested in this sort of atypical travel. In 2004, looking for a way to elevate the brand's awareness and add differentiation to its experience without losing its core focus on authentic eco-experiences, Lindblad Expeditions embarked on one of the travel industry's most important strategic alliances, joining forces with *National Geographic* to dramatically strengthen the experience it could offer customers. By adding the deep expertise and gravitas of *National Geographic*'s scientists, explorers, naturalists, and photographers to its cruises, Lindblad Expeditions created a dramatically differentiated traveler experience.

While other cruise lines could likely add a naturalist or photographer, they could not match the depth of knowledge provided by *National Geographic* employees sharing their expertise with travelers. Today, Lindblad Expeditions-National Geographic operates its own fleet of ten ships, offering life-changing experiences on all seven continents.

Lindblad Expeditions identified untapped audiences for the type of travel it offered. Its move to partner with *National Geographic* was a matter of "playing golf," keeping an eye on the consumers it wanted to attract. When I spoke to Richard Fontaine, former CMO of Lindblad Expeditions, a few years back, he told me about the genesis for this partnership and why it was a win-win for both organizations.

When Sven initiated the conversation with *National Geographic* . . . he was looking for a way to elevate our awareness and simultaneously enhance the guest experience. By aligning with *National Geographic*, it allowed us to bring the organization's content, information, and educational programs—authentic, real-life explorers and naturalists—into our guest experience. Among the most obvious examples is that on every one of our expeditions, we have certified photo instructors who have been trained by the photographers who are published in *National Geographic* magazine. They are at the top of their profession, and you're working side by side with them to improve your own photography skills.[13]

"More than this," said Fontaine,

the *National Geographic* alliance has allowed us to create a much more enhanced focus on environmental conservation and sustainability in the areas in which we travel. We are trying to leave the places we visit in better condition than when we started traveling so future generations will have the same opportunity to see them. Obviously, there is no better partner for us than *National Geographic*. They have a field staff on the ground all the time, doing research to try to protect and preserve these places.[14]

There is no better partner for Lindblad Expeditions than *National Geographic* for another reason. The National Geographic Society is still perceived as a leading authority on issues of geographic knowledge and information. Its association with Lindblad Expeditions has brought enormous benefit to both organizations. Whereas Lindblad Expeditions was once the only show in town—if you wanted to go to the Galápagos Islands or the Antarctic, you went with Lindblad—now there are multiple companies to choose from, so drawing a distinction that puts you ahead of the pack is necessary.

Where *National Geographic* is able to expand its brand by reminding people that it defines ecological, preservation, and nature exploration and that all who come after it are mere pretenders, so, too, does Lindblad Expeditions offer the kind of experience that only a group so focused on the quality of the adventure, the potential for expanding your horizons, can provide. When I spoke with Noah Brodsky, Lindblad's chief commercial officer, this was the point he emphasized. By connecting with *National Geographic*, Lindblad Expeditions added to its reputation as the groundbreaker in ecotourism, bringing the words and pictures within the *National Geographic* magazine's iconic yellow border to life. Sven Lindblad knew what his brand stood for and shifted in a way that added more power and authenticity to the brand's simple idea. Other cruise lines can hire photographers and naturalists, but Lindblad Expeditions lets you travel with the experienced photographers and naturalists from *National Geographic*, experts in wildlife, the oceans, and the rain forests. It was a way for Lindblad Expeditions to dramatically differentiate itself in the sea of cruise and travel companies.[15]

Thinking creatively about how your business intersects with or shares the spirit of another is part of what makes joining forces such an intriguing opportunity. Can you find a partner with whom you can join forces in order to create a more engaging and interesting experience that takes two ordinary experiences or products and creates something extraordinary?

The process of examining what you do in relationship to what another organization does, to come together in a way that strengthens both and that highlights the best of what each does, is one that will leave you with a deeper understanding of what you do. And all businesses benefit from knowing what, precisely, they do—what they do well and what might be best left to others. What does your business do that could benefit from the addition of alternative delivery systems, expanded options, or increased levels of service, all without adding to your own bottom line or expanding the human resources dedicated to delivering them? Look for ways that joining forces can be the path to the proverbial "one plus one equals three."

Lens 4

SEE LIKE A CONCIERGE

The "see like a concierge" lens is about being that someone with the expertise and ability to listen and solve problems better and faster than the average person can on their own, even after hours of research. As with everything, there are different levels of what is generally called concierge service, the quality of which will, without a doubt, vary. This chapter is not a review site, so this isn't about who, specifically, executes such service better. I use the word "concierge" because of its association with high-end hotels and properties and all of the expectations they inspire.

Concierge service is more than individualized service. It requires an informed person with the emotional intelligence to take an idea, question, or service through a logical progression that a customer might not have thought of, never mind expect. Concierge remains a valid service model, and this is especially true as younger generations are more open to identifying the assistance they need and looking for those who have the expertise to fill that need.

What constitutes the concierge experience? The good concierge uses all the fields of vision: tunnel, peripheral, and wrap-around—and does so knowingly. They ask and, more importantly, listen. They hear both what is said and, at times, what is notably left unsaid.

When I arrange to go to a shop in a neighborhood with which I'm less familiar and mention it as an offhand remark, I don't expect anything from the person listening to me. But when that person responds, "While you're waiting for your car repair to finish, there's a great cafe with Wi-Fi around the corner that serves one of my favorite sandwiches. Sometimes, I take my food to the park down the street; have you seen the new sculptures there?" I feel a human connection that didn't require much. This could just be the random, chatty clerk. Or this could be a business that encourages its workers to engage with customers, to take a few extra minutes, to make sure their experience feels like more than a drive-by.

The conceit of a concierge is the removal of friction from a customer's experience. A simple idea, right? Think about it at the most mundane level. How hard is it to find your product? Can you look it up online or find it on a shelf? If a purchase is dependent on someone who has no fealty to your specific brand or item, you are likely losing customers you never knew you could have. It's not a matter of whether one person buys your product on a given day—a lifetime of purchasing may have already slipped through your fingers. A smooth buying experience today leads to a repeat purchase that becomes a habit tomorrow.

One name that is synonymous with ease of use, putting customer experience first, and putting a dash (or more) of the concierge spirit into everything he does, in all his many businesses, is restaurateur Danny Meyer. If you do a quick Google search for "What is Danny Meyer's hiring philosophy," you'll get a few pages (or more) of some version of: "Hiring employees with a high HQ score is what really tips the scales in terms of company culture, and a happy staff will always provide a better experience for customers."[1] As Meyer himself has put it, "You distinguish yourself first and foremost by picking your team even better than the other guy. And I always felt that would be our advantage."[2] HQ is Meyer-speak for "Hospitality Quotient." Meyer has a list of six things he looks for in his future employees that he believes indicate a candidate's aptitude for providing hospitable service. Figuring out your organization's equivalent of that ability to provide exceptional customer service is, of course, the key.

What are the qualities you look for in those you bring into your corporate fold? This isn't a casual question. It's one that you and your leadership team need to spend some time on and work out to a highly detailed degree. It will be the key to your vision, to how your vision is executed—and, most importantly, it will draw the most direct line between your idea or product and how you serve your customers in a way that exceeds their expectations.

MAKING REPAIRS AND MAKING A LIFELONG CUSTOMER

As was the case for so many during the COVID-19 pandemic, stuck at home, I did more home repairs than I had previously. The reason I hadn't done many home repairs before then was in part because I didn't have the time. It was also because, despite being relatively handy, I am not particularly careful and am not a big fan of reading instructions. In other words, I can make simple tasks harder, which often requires things needing to be redone.

These projects were a tremendous challenge. But before I would head out to my local Ace Hardware store, Chubby's Hardware, for what I'd need, I would send the store pictures of what needed to be done. The owner would review the photos, call me back, and not only have the parts waiting for me when I got to the store but also show me how to use what he was selling to me, what tools I would need, and what to do if something didn't go as planned. They were, in no uncertain terms, private lessons in, for example, how to fix a leaky sink or a dimmer switch. All of a sudden, the hardware store was no longer just a place to pick things up and maybe ask a question. It was a store whose owner was a personal concierge showing me how to fix home things, well beyond selling me the parts and tools. It was the kind of pivot that reflected an understanding of what was needed and what it could offer, and the store offered the kind of concierge service that made sense for a given time and place.

This is the kind of service that produces a devoted customer. Recently, I called this concierge-like owner to see if I had left my credit card there when I'd stopped by the previous day. "No," he reported, but he tried to be helpful: "Where did you go after you left me?" I admitted that I had stopped into the gas station down the block, but they weren't answering the phone. The owner then walked over to the gas station, found my card, and held onto it until I could come back the following weekend.

The boundaries between service and marketing are blurred. Most companies have staff who interact with customers. What those interactions entail—how a few more minutes with a customer can turn a one-time visitor into a committed client—is what's crucial. The concierge-thinking employees are aware that providing a service that takes the full range of vision into account is one that leaves a consumer feeling seen, understood, and served in a way that is satisfying and, more importantly, that leaves competitors to pale in comparison.

Certain companies and business leaders are well known for bringing this sentiment to all that they do: the Four Seasons hotels, Danny Meyer restaurants, Nordstrom. In all cases, when these brands arise, they employ a smooth process in which all customers engage with a clear goal of satisfaction and ease of use, a process that makes customers relax. The consumers of such organizations feel understood before they open their mouths, and they rest assured that every effort will be made to expand on their positive experience in such a way that it is worth going out of one's way to find these companies above all others.

THE GENIUS OF SERVICE AT THE GENIUS BAR

The growing preponderance of companies that have found success by offering services above and beyond mere products establishes the growth of the service economy as real. Apple's Genius Bar is a signature example of how the company embraces the spirit of concierge service. From the ground up, the experience the Genius Bar provides is about access, transparency, and availability, from the layout to the plentiful places to sit, to the lovely wood furniture, to the visible blue shirts that denote "Ask me!" Apple Geniuses might ask, "While you're here, do you know how to use this cool feature on your iPhone? Did you know that you can get a longer battery life from your phone if you switch your apps to this setting, like this? Allow me to show you how you can keep as many photos as you'd like—but if you do it off your phone, you'll save your memory."

There is no line of purchasers snaking their way from a single cash register; anyone walking around with the right shirt can sell you what you want to buy. From a customer point of view, Apple removed the points of friction and looked for ways to create a strong and pleasant sales experience. It went above and beyond the typical 80/20 (looking for one or two bits of an experience to make your signature—the points about which you expect customers to talk and share and rave about) and went even bigger. Not only does this ease improve a customer's experience and increase the likelihood of their return, but, especially in the day and age of social media, it also produces an experience worthy of being shared. That which is shareable is either terrifically good or exceptionally bad—whichever it is, it's extraordinary in some way. Concierge-type service places the experience you offer on the *terrific* end of that spectrum.

We see in so many ways how important experiences are to driving happiness. Products make life easier, but experiences make life *better*. When we talk of the concierge experience, of finding ways to bring happiness to the consumer experience and make that part of (or the entirety of) what you offer, we're responding to the cultural shift that appreciates experience over stuff. Not only do we want the extraordinary experience; we are coming to see the value in what that experience offers us, such that we see the benefits as worth spending money to obtain. Yes, you could do it yourself—whatever it is—but is that how you want to spend your time? All of a sudden, we are a culture that is conscious of the value of our time.

Cassie Holmes, a professor at UCLA's Anderson School of Management whose specialty is, of all things, happiness, conducted a study that explored happiness in light of the importance of time versus money. The value of your time can be measured in how it frees you up to do things that are worthwhile and important to you, whether in fact or in theory. Holmes teaches a course to MBA candidates about applying the science of happiness to life design to focus more of our time on living happier lives. As she explained to me, "When you focus on time rather than money with respect to how you wouldn't pay for the products, then those products become more reflective of you—because the way we spend our time is reflective of ourselves."[3]

She explained that while focusing on time is better for happiness and our satisfaction with products, people tend to focus instead on money. In a study where she asked Americans if they'd prefer to have more time or more money, most said they would prefer more money. But, in that same study, Holmes found that those who valued time over money lived significantly happier lives, even controlling for how much time and money participants had.

The cultural shift from money to time as the more valuable entity is one of breaking habits of thought. The quantifiability of the value of money is much easier to assess, but the extent to which you can provide products that ask customers to value their time more than their money, that help them use their time better, is where you'll find your customers. The shift is already taking place. "Ten years ago, I actually had a hard time finding examples from the . . . marketing landscape of brands that focus on time; now, they're everywhere," said Holmes. "Increasingly, brands are aware that consumers are time-poor, so the [more that] you can offer something that allows them to be less time-poor, more time-affluent, the better."[4]

CONCIERGES DO MORE THAN MAKE DINNER RESERVATIONS

Regardless of the sense in which you are using it, concierge service is many steps beyond just making it easy for you to choose a product. Retail has long known the power of a personal shopper. The furniture store already recognizes that the successful salesperson knows more than what materials were used to make the chair and how long it will take to deliver a piece with a certain upholstery. It knows that the successful salesperson can look at pictures of rooms, listen to a customer describe their likes and dislikes, and advise them in a way that feels substantive. Concierge service is more than this, however. It is a quest for the best of what we can offer with a goal of surfacing the best in customers. It is the pursuit of the nobility of service. In the words of the Ritz-Carlton Hotel Company (fashioned by founder Horst Schulze), it is the manifestation of "ladies and gentlemen serving ladies and gentlemen."[5] In 2022 language, it is one person—the concierge—seeing who the customer before them is and responding above and beyond what their job may dictate. It is recognizing the need to know about things to do in the neighborhood next to the glasses shop because there are typically a few hours to kill while waiting for glasses to be prepared. It's about someone seeing the person standing before them and recommending something they would like rather than the generic choice offered by a quick Google search.

I've been fortunate in my life to have been pampered by a few concierge experiences in hotels and resorts. The very accommodating people behind these experiences go beyond answering questions or solving problems by handing you an AI-generated list of restaurants or local activities. They listen, and they observe. They watch the choices I make (or don't) and then advise in a highly individualized manner, combining graciousness and professionalism to create an experience that delights because it is, in fact, exactly what I wanted to do without even knowing it—and also because they devoted more time and thought than I expected them to.

How can your business encourage real-time human interactions with your customers that approximates this type of concierge service? How are these moments facilitated not at the expense of reaching a broader audience but in the name of reaching a broader audience?

Interestingly, not only will thinking like a concierge offer a superior level of service to your customers with which it will be hard to compete; it will also serve to establish a dynamic that will make the inevitable difficulties in customer service far more manageable. With attention, with a few extra steps taken to assure satisfaction, comes not only brand loyalty but also brand understanding. I am far more willing to accept human error when a company has served me well, shown gratitude for the choice I've made in coming to them, and established itself as an organization seeking to do right and well by its customers.

I am also more likely to share about such a company on social media, spontaneously act as a walking five-star review, and otherwise spread the word about my positive experience. This is true when this kind of company goes the extra mile for me, but it's also true when a hiccup occurs and the outcome is less than ideal. In both cases, there is an opportunity to connect with consumers because today's customers are far more aware of what it takes to create a good customer experience.

A CLOSER LOOK: A MASSIVE TRANSFORMATION FROM PRODUCT TO EXPERIENCE: FORD

There are few places where the words "concierge" and "experience" are farther apart than the car dealership. To bring the concierge spirit to an industry that is as entrenched as the car-buying experience is to take on a behemoth, no hyperbole included.

Looking back decades or even just to last year, the view is largely the same. Car manufacturers are companies that make products built by engineers. Marketing efforts by those companies are about selling those products. Dealers are about distributing those products. In other words, the car companies never come near the customer—if by "customer" you mean the driver.

When I spoke with Suzy Deering, former global CMO at Ford, she told me that she didn't care about the ways things had always been done. Years ago, she saw that Ford never spoke to customers. When the company created ads and websites or promoted itself, it spoke of what its engineers had created: the car. There is nothing wrong with this per se, but in an age when corporate responsibility and responsiveness loom large and the consumer has a voice that is loud and clear on social-media platforms, failing to communicate with your ultimate customer, said Deering, felt like a big mistake.

It's true that customers did occasionally hear from the car company. When their warranty was about to run out, Ford would reach out to sell them an extension. When something went wrong, they'd hear about a recall. But this wasn't communicating, and Deering saw this with a clarity that convinced her that something needed to change. She stepped forward to say, "We are not in the business of moving chunks of metal from our factories to our dealerships and hoping they land in someone's garage. We need to take a longer view. We need to speak to experience. We see experience as a growing and important part of what makes people act: to buy, to share about their experience, to repeat that act of buying."

With a new management team at Ford, Deering developed and set about enacting a bold, audacious mission of shifting the goal of the company. Up until then, the car-buying experience had been dominated by the dealership; it had been, until recently, Ford's real customer. And the brand–dealership dynamic is an interesting one. First and foremost, like most automobile companies, Ford does not own its dealerships. But they are the ones on Main Street, engaging with the people Ford wanted behind the wheel of its cars. And there really aren't a lot of positives that come with the dealership experience other than being located on Main Street. Ask a lot of people to describe the car-buying experience, and the word you'll hear quite a bit is "atrocious."

In the traditional dynamic, you go into your local dealership and meet someone on the sales team. Their objective is to sell you a hunk of metal (that is, a car). They don't know much about you, but maybe they'll try to learn a bit. But, typically, the relationship is lopsided. You are likely to be the educated consumer who has done her research online and read reviews and who knows what price range to expect. In this day and age, very few walk in cold and say, "Tell me about your car and why I should buy it."

You want to hear about the details you *don't* have; you want the information the salesperson has. But they aren't interested in building a relationship with you. Once you buy (or don't buy), they will never see you again. They know that if they let you walk away without buying a car, you are going to go to a different dealership and, perhaps, respond better to their spiel. And every salesperson knows that you close the deal with someone standing in front of you. It's also often hard to compare cars because, even between dealerships of the same company, different models are on the floor and different bells and whistles are on offer.

The experience is, in a word and at best, transactional. At worst, it's a hard sell that no one enjoys and everyone wishes hadn't taken place at all. During a recent conversation I had with Bob Pittman, cofounder of MTV and current CEO of iHeartMedia, he uttered the wishful thinking that so many car buyers think at some point in the process: "When I start looking for a car, my immediate thought is, 'Oh my God, do I really want to go through all that?' What would I give to have somebody I trust go and look at all the cars? 'You want to look at the BMW? Three choices?' Yes. 'Here's the car for you.' Yes, again, and thank you."[6]

You buy the car. It's as if the salesperson never existed. Your next experience is service. A different person steps up; they get to know you a little bit if they are a good service manager. But, again, the experience is largely transactional. If you're lucky and the brand you go with is of a certain level of luxury, the first service is provided by the dealership. After that, however, the sticker shock that is service through the dealership is a hard pill to swallow. The price–value relationship is so out of whack, you often end up paying twice what you would pay your local gas station for an oil change. It is hard—even with luxury, white-glove service—to argue that there is enough value to justify the exponential increase in cost by staying with the dealership. Your relationship with the car brand could be quite brief. And even when it isn't and you stick with the dealership for service, it isn't meaningful.

This reminds me of a time, many years ago, when I and my young family were on a family visit in New Jersey. Our car was five years old (out of warranty) but had only thirty thousand miles on it. But this was a German luxury car. For that kind of car, I considered thirty thousand miles a still-new car. And because it was a luxury car, I had certain expectations that I would be treated as someone who has opted for the higher-end version of things—say, a nice hotel—and that when I would interact with the dealership I could expect, yes, a concierge experience.

As we drove toward home in our station wagon, the red lights suddenly lit up, and then the car just stopped. The failure was, in a word, significant. It was a failure in the suspension system, which meant the car could not be driven at all, not even to a local service station. So I tried calling Mercedes. It was a Sunday afternoon, and, not surprisingly, no one picked up. I tried the in-car service speaker, which is used to request roadside service. An operator nowhere near offered to arrange for a tow truck to come from who-knows-where, but this was no concierge service. There was no special relationship with the towing company. There was also no attempt to find a place to which the car could be towed that would actually help me get it fixed. I ended up having the car towed to a dealership in South Jersey, leaving me with a bit of a mobility problem. And this is where Mercedes signed off.

On my own, I took a taxi to a car-rental place at a local airport and drove back to New York City. It was, to say the least, not an easy experience. And it did not get easier. I waited for an assessment, an estimate (which was exorbitant), and then the repair itself to be completed. It required all my powers of persuasion and haranguing to convince the dealer to ultimately deliver my car to me in the city.

What I thought would happen didn't happen. What Deering described to me more recently is more in line with what I'd expected all those many years ago. Ford's roadside assistance will now send the tow truck, but it will also arrange for the loaner car. This will happen even when Ford is not open because Ford has a relationship with local rental-car companies. Even when you are out of warranty, Ford will stand behind its product and will treat you the same regardless. Listening to Deering describe this, I could only nod my head and think, *Finally*.

I don't think what I expected from my very high-end luxury brand was so outrageous. I expected a seamless, frictionless experience. When my car broke down and I had to coordinate its care from two hundred miles away, I was a person with a big job, a young family, and finite time to spend with them. And I expected more than just a shiny metal box when I made my purchase.

When you think of concierge service, your mind immediately jumps to a hotel, and for good reason. A hotel is probably the first time most hear the word, and it's even more likely that it's the first place most people have seen someone wearing a button declaring this to be their purpose. Bringing the spirit of a good hotel concierge to the car industry is no easy task. Everything about the industry has customers convinced that they should not expect it and the people selling to and servicing them convinced that it isn't necessary to offer it. That being said, there are certain advantages the car industry has over hotels, of course. Unlike the hotel concierge, whose clients are unknown, with preferences and expectations that vary from person to person, a car dealership lives where its customers live. And it doesn't need to sell those customers cars all day long, every day; it just needs to do it once per customer and then again in a reasonably protracted amount of time.

When Deering started to think of bringing the concierge mentality and level of service to Ford, she, too, thought of hotels. Basic hospitality. The kind that is offered consistently, regardless of location. Translated to the car scenario, she intended to change a well-known dynamic that goes something like this: You buy your car from a dealership. Anything you try to do at another dealer is going to be a hard slog. You want to get your car serviced, but there are no appointments available when you need one. They don't know you. Your car breaks down in a town other than your own, but there is no impetus for them to treat you well, hustle you in, make it easy for the service to be done, offer a ride or a loaner—because they will never see you again. There is no future sale down the line, and you didn't buy your car there. Local dealerships offer locals better prices because they are more likely to be the ones to return to buy another car in three to five years.

In her quest to promote the concierge spirit, Deering took a radical approach to speak to the very DNA of Ford, its purpose, which Deering describes as "to help build a better world where every person is free to move and pursue their dreams. That is why we exist." She continued, "So all of those decisions are from where the company's purpose was, [which] drives every decision we make about the company from a brand perspective. It led us to this concept and idea that we build trusted products and services that help to engage lives every day. And that's through passion. That's through authenticity because that's the human side of us. That's through purposeful ingenuity. And [it's] also effortless."[7]

And Deering thought about how hotel chains use their prolific presence in multiple communities to be a positive presence in order to integrate their purpose into every way a customer interacts with them. For her, she thought specifically of Marriott. As a long-time executive, she's logged a lot of miles and stayed in a lot of hotel rooms. As she explained to me, "If you're going to have a relationship, you have to be more like Marriott than General Motors, in terms of listening and empowering the frontline."[8]

The challenge to shift the company's thinking was tremendous. Deering was facing down decades of rather fixed ideas about what salespeople are there to do. In the service department, it is to sell as many tune-ups, upgraded as much as possible—to sell you the most expensive bike rack, not the one that responds to what you've said you need. Historically, it has not been there to solve your mobility problems; it's there to sell you as much as it can.

Deering described the shift to me as one from where Ford was mostly about making great cars—which she still believes is one of the major points and about which she has enormous pride —to one where it started seeing *drivers* as its customers rather than the dealerships, regardless of its sales source. As Deering explained to me,

> We have to focus a lot more on ownership. And where do we create that, the ultimate ecosystem that you connect into? How do we fit into your lifestyle? And that means thinking differently about the vehicle in the sense of it being more than the actual metal itself. Where's all the connectivity from technology from a data perspective? What now creates interactions every day with the Ford brand? And that is a massive departure because before, the everyday interactions would have been just with the shipment. We are bringing the customer to tuck back into the family board.[9]

Taking a page from hotels and other industries that rely on ongoing relationships, Deering developed a Ford mobile app, putting power in the hands of the consumer to ask for and coordinate what they want and when they want it, whereas in the past they were at the mercy of what the dealership may or may not be willing to provide. For the first time, Ford has built a digital team.

On the app, you have the ability to book appointments based not on some vestigial relationship with the specific sales source but on what is easiest for you. If you want to buy your car on the app, "with about nine clicks you can purchase and arrange to pick it up at the dealership of your choice. Very easy. No friction."[10] If you want to service your car five towns over because that's where your kid's orthodontist is, you have the same access to appointments as those who live in that town. If you want to have the first service appointment of the day and it's worth driving a little more to get it, you can do that. Maybe you want to be picked up, or maybe you want the car to be picked up and delivered somewhere else—all that can be done as well. The app embodies frictionless communication and interaction from the get-go.

In order to bring concierge service, you have to make access to service easy. Deering saw the extent to which concierge service is far easier to provide when the technology is there to make it possible. And she understands the limits of what tech can provide and where the human factor is vital.

> We still believe there has to be a human involved. It's a pretty fascinating data point about which we did some testing. Even if you go through a buying experience on an e-commerce site and they think it's fantastic and wonderful that with very few very easy steps you can get to a purchase, customers still want somebody they can call and ask a question to. Or, they still want to be able to go into a dealership—but not to be sold to, just to ask a couple of questions.[11]

Bringing the human component on board means there needs to be a lot of dealer network education. Some may already be providing concierge-level (or close to it) service, but the point is to achieve a level of consistency and to establish expectations across the brand. Ford wants to help them make the transition, knowing some "will gracefully make the shift; others won't." Deering keeps in mind her relationship with Marriott, what she refers to as their "bond." But she sees the ways the Marriott app doesn't work and wants to stay on top of how the Ford app evolves and reflects user experiences.

A CLOSER LOOK: HELPING EMPLOYEES STAY ON TOP OF THEIR LIVES AND GET THEIR JOB DONE: SODEXO

Sometimes the services that constitute concierge experiences are about one business helping the people who work in another business live their lives more easily. One such example: Sodexo's Circles Concierge.

Sodexo is an international company with offerings that range from food-service operations, including staff restaurants, catering, executive dining, vending, and meal delivery, to integrated facilities-management services that include both soft services (reception, concierge, cleaning, pantry, laundry, groundskeeping, waste management, vendor management, etc.) and hard services (HVAC systems, electrical systems including substations up to 220kV, energy efficiency and sustainability, plumbing/water treatment, plant/sewage treatment, plant operation, annual equipment operation and maintenance contracts, project management, etc.). In other words, it services businesses of enormous variety and understands a lot of the inner workings of how those companies work.[12]

Given the range of services Sodexo offers and the equally wide range of business to which it offers those services, it was a stroke of brilliance that it recognized how much more help it could be to its client companies. And so Circles Concierge was formed, offering highly trained concierges to respond to "every need, from running the simplest errands to satisfying complex, time-consuming requests," on behalf of client company employees. Circles offers solutions around the clock for any kind of service, from getting a last-minute travel visa to dropping a car off at a mechanic. The idea is to do for the employee so that the employee can stay at and focus on work.

The nitty-gritty of the concept is itself offered in a concierge model. That is, if a company wants to provide services and support for its employees, that company can define what that might mean. A company perk that clearly benefits the company—in worker focus, retention, and satisfaction—but only if executed well. In the case of Sodexo, it originated the service knowing that it would need to help the mid-level executive but also the factory worker. The difference? One has a computer in front of them all day and has no trouble quickly looking up and performing quick tasks online; the factory or oil-rig worker, given where they spend their work day, can't do the same.

Providing these services requires technology, access to data about the employees (without prompting any privacy concerns), and a lot more, like understanding what the range of requests might be, plus staffing that allows you to offer 24/7 support with multiple ways to engage, be it phone, email, or text. And, of course, making sure employees know about the service and understand that its use is part of their payment package, and having successful enough encounters that they return to use the service again—not to mention the all-important share. Nothing says "success" like an Instagram post raving about what a great help your service was.

Ronni Schorr, Circles's global vice president of marketing and strategy, talked with me about the challenges these types of programs face, starting with the word "concierge," which often comes across as snooty and doesn't resonate with a large number or variety of the employees they hope to help. As she explained, it is that variety to which they must respond:

> P&G had factory workers, they had middle managers, and they had executives. To be honest, the factory workers were the most demanding, and they were the ones where their productivity was very important. If they couldn't get razor blades out, they couldn't sell razor blades, right? We offered solutions to those factory workers, but we didn't call it "concierge." We called it "personal assistants." The willingness to participate starts with the name.[13]

She also spoke to me about how to create a team of concierges who will live up to the promises the service makes.

> Training, depending on level, takes two to four weeks, and it was heavy-duty training. Part of it was the Ritz-Carlton training program. The Ritz-Carlton has a training program that they license out. This is how, from the moment you walk into one of their hotels, somebody knows your name, and when it's clear what your preferred name is, that, too, is shared with the rest of the staff. And those preferences are saved and shared, so no matter which hotel you go to, they know you.[14]

Schorr described to me how well Circles has embraced the concierge model. It isn't enough to book a table at a restaurant for the marketing manager. They're going to look at your LinkedIn profile, and if you offer them, they'll also use your other social-media accounts to offer more than what you asked for. The concierges can point out the exhibit that's happening near the restaurant where you're going. Not only is that a service anyone would be thrilled to receive; it's the kind of help a person talks about and shares about.

"The younger generation—the Gen Zs, the millennials—they have no issue about giving personal information as long as they get something in return."[15] So the younger generation is more open to using concierge services, wanting the services, sharing about the services, and seeing a company that offers the services as one for which they want to work.

Clearly, Circles has tapped into something. "Interestingly, hotels are contacting us for their employees, even though they are themselves hospitality companies. They wanted us to run their front of house for their corporate headquarters—because they saw the importance, but they didn't have the staff."[16]

A CLOSER LOOK: THE TANGLED WEB THAT IS HEALTH CARE

I think often of a *Seinfeld* bit in which Jerry Seinfeld holds forth about waiting rooms. The very name of these rooms makes clear the intention to keep you waiting. Watching people join you inside causes a kind of anxiety and tension, and, when you are finally called in, an absurd amount of pride can swell up despite the fact that you've done nothing worthy of feeling this way.[17]

The concept of medical concierge services is one of the easier to imagine and one that has been around for quite some time, as evidenced by Seinfeld riffing on what was then already a long-known trope. As insurance companies became increasingly labyrinthian, draconian, and miserly, there have long been alternatives for those who can pay extreme amounts of money to skip the line, leave forms behind, and not be beholden to the random approvals of a non–health practitioner about their medical treatment. What has changed more recently, as we've discussed throughout this chapter, is access and expectation. That is, the ease of access, simplifying of bureaucracy, and emphasis on medical people making medical decisions have expanded enormously. This is now something that is packaged and sold to mere mortals.

The concierge service isn't just about how smoothly the appointment booking goes. There are real issues of medical care involved. Having made your way through the phone prompts, accepted the appointment time that required you to take time away from work, and waited longer than you wanted to for that appointment day to arrive, you finally get to the examination and . . . if you sneeze, you could miss the doctor's time there. The number of minutes allocated to a given patient is infinitesimal, and this isn't just your sense of things. Google will turn up hundreds of articles outlining in great detail the demands put on doctors to shove as many patients into as few minutes as possible.

Furthermore, the doctor that comes into your room addresses only the most immediate issue, and nary a word is exchanged outside of that. The splinter in your foot is infected, so the doctor arrives, takes it out, prescribes an antibiotic ointment, tells you not to walk on it, and, as soon as you take a breath, turns to leave. There's no "How are you?" or inquiry about whether there is anything else you might have concerns about or to follow up on a matter discussed in previous appointments. This system fails to address you as a whole person and how you could live your life in a healthier manner. This problem–solution approach is so focused on a single symptom at a time that the idea of a whole person is completely lost.

Taking this on in the form of a medical concierge is a rapidly growing approach that takes the concierge concept and adds a subscription element. The typical dynamic is one where you pay in advance and know that, when you need it, you will get (for some several thousands of dollars) a doctor's time and attention. In exchange for this willingness to put a deposit down, you'll get a conversation about your life, eating habits, overall health, how your exercise routine is going (or not), and so on. Doctors will be willing to spend time with your whole self, not just the part that happens to ail at that moment. The expectation becomes the relationship that used to exist between doctor and patient—that, over time, they will get to know you and so will understand that you got that splinter because you have a house with an aging deck that has caused you all sorts of trouble. In such a system, because you pay in advance at a rate that exceeds insurance reimbursements, the doctor can afford to spend that time with you.

So, while it is a nice branding term—"concierge" medical services—it doesn't really conform to what we traditionally think of with that word. These services are trying—offering services that are helplines for taking full advantage of services and directing clients to specific practitioners to help in wading through the undifferentiated list of participating doctors—but no one is pretending that they're forming ongoing relationships.

One aspect of the medical-care universe that has some semblance of the concierge are those hospitals that serve a significant number of out-of-town patients. If you are traveling for medical care and head for the Mayo Clinic, the Cleveland Clinic, NewYork-Presbyterian, you will have available to you a hospital concierge who will assist you in finding places for your family to stay or to find ways for you to coordinate any outpatient care you might need. They will also provide orienting information (transportation, parking validation, food—both in the neighborhood and what can be delivered into the hospital—etc.) in order to help the new to town navigate their way. They have certain qualities that feel like those of a hotel concierge; they smooth out and even anticipate the problems one might face. And for those who are traveling internationally, hospitals have a team of staff who will help with the increasingly complicated logistics of being strangers arriving in a new place with the worries and distractions of doing so for a medical procedure.

In the case of Mayo Clinic and NewYork-Presbyterian, the concierge pages of their websites make clear how focused they are on providing these services. The help Mayo lists includes assistance in navigating its portal; choosing a hotel; identifying food, banks, medical supplies, and hairdressers in the new city; finding recreational spots to check out during downtime; securing child or adult care; and, of course, obtaining notary services. NewYork-Presbyterian adds to that list and offers itinerary planning, appointments with people who can help explain medical reports and directions, coordination of at-home care, and recommendations for "lifestyle modification for health promotion."

When we look at these services offered as a matter of course and compare them with those that are membership based, you see a theme that mostly shines a bright light on what normal medical care is failing to do as a matter of routine. Since this is not a book about the woes of the US health care system, we'll leave that for others to tackle. For our purposes here, there are lessons to be learned for those who are interested in looking at their own business and looking at everything that is wrong with it.

Wrong? Really? Yes.

Look at your business or industry and ask yourself: What are those parts of the way you do business that are "necessary evils"? What do your customers accept despite it being less than what you yourself would accept as a quality of service? Even better, ask: In what way is your industry or business meeting minimums instead of achieving best practices?

Medical concierge services start at the very beginning of the process in tackling the problematic aspects of their business. They create sign-ups and initial portals that make it easy for you to tell your new medical provider a lot about yourself without feeling as if you had to write your own memoir. They shrink call wait times by making more resources available on websites and through portals but also by shelling out for more operators during high-traffic times. They build in ways to communicate with doctors that systematize responses, establish a direct line for seeking clarity about lab results, and coordinate referrals so you end up where you need to go and they understand why you've come.

Distinguishing between the problem-directed versus the care-directed medical attention that one receives starts with a very straightforward question: "How are you today?" Does the doctor asking it actually pause to hear your response? Is there space for you to think, *How am I?* The opportunity to respond with something like "I know I'm here for the splinter infection, but I've also had a worrisome pang of pain in my stomach for a few weeks" is now something of a luxury.

The most important part of incorporating concierge–like service is realizing, first, that it's a big promise. We can all use Google and Yelp or get guidance from TikTok and Twitter. When it comes to capturing someone's business and retaining it, the bar is far higher than that. What people want is quality, and they want someone to save them time in getting that quality. Like a great chief of staff or a great assistant, what you want is someone who will understand you well enough to know what you need slightly before you know you need it and who will be ready with the solution by the time you finish posing the question.

If you can do that for any category—in a world where the most precious commodity is not just saving someone time and trouble but also leaving them with the feeling that you did something they would never have done otherwise—you'll have a hit on your hands. Providing a concierge-level experience is a big ask that is incredibly difficult to deliver but will exponentially increase your value.

Lens 5

GO THE RENTAL ROUTE

When I think of my own personal experience with the concept of "going rental," I don't have to go too far back. This past fall, my wife and I dropped my daughter off for her first year of college. As we made our way through the streets of Ann Arbor, Michigan, in our rented SUV, we made stop after stop, procuring the items that would render her dorm room her new home away from home. Most parents who have sent children to college know the mental arithmetic I was doing: How much does she need? What will fit in her (very typically sized) dorm room? I found myself wondering if I could rent a dorm-sized refrigerator and microwave that could be delivered to her room at the start of the term and whisked away at the end. Renting would be much easier than buying them, storing them (for which I'd also pay), and moving them (ditto) when she would, more likely than not, change rooms and spaces enough the following year that much of what we purchased wouldn't be useful again.

There are so many moments, days, and stages of life that require things we will not need to own once that moment, day, or stage ends. There are hobbies that are best approached with temporary tools before a commitment to ownership is made. There are needs that arise once a year—and never more often—for which a space, a thing, or a service is required that immediately becomes a burden to own when the need goes away.

Hilti has disrupted the market for construction tools by shifting from a purchase- to a transaction/rental-based business model. It realized that its customers' need is not just to own a reliable tool but to have the right tool at the right time. Hilti's customers simply rent whatever tool they need, whenever they need it, rather than having to own every single tool they might possibly need in their personal stock.

How does one examine a preexisting corporate structure and look for ways to engage customers in this different way? Break down what you do and offer; see where a one-time sale can turn into a repeated, ephemeral engagement; and then maintain that relationship by understanding all the steps necessary to provide that service or tool, including how to present the options available, identify the segments of availability, offer choices within categories that speak to the range of needs customers might want (whether they know it or not), provide access to those choices and arrange for their return, and, most importantly, guarantee a working service or tool and make efficient the efforts needed to address when there is a breakdown of said service or tool.

The shift this offering makes in customer experience is profound. People simply don't automatically assume that ownership is the first line of defense when addressing a need in their lives. For some, this is political. There is a movement to produce, have, and throw out less. For others, it's about Marie Kondo–ing their lives, and renting allows them to reap the benefits of a product without needing to find a place for it in their home when they're done. There are economic reasons. It is always going to cost less to rent something once than to buy it and use it once. And there are reasons that have to do with the speed with which improvements to tools are made. A company can do well to lease computers, knowing they will be used hard and well for two years and that they'll be replaced at the point when their efficacy and ability to stay updated begins to decline.

TRAINS, PLANES, AND AUTOMOBILES . . . AND SCOOTERS AND MOPEDS

Whether with bicycles, motorized scooters, mopeds, or cars, the transportation sector has defined the ways in which recognizing that ownership is not only unnecessary but is also, in fact, a burden can create an entirely new market and new experience of what has been with us for a long time. The garage full of mechanized objects that are used twice a year regularly—or used four times and then forgotten—and the garage that contains vehicles you want to use but have nowhere to store once you've arrived at your destination make it clear why this is the case.

Many entrepreneurs are attaining remarkable success by looking through the lens of going the rental route—looking at opportunities to rent a product or service for a specific period of time and eliminating all the negative factors of ownership. It's not that it's a new idea (consider Rent the Runway, the various maternity formal-wear rental options that have existed since the '90s, etc.), but recent technology has created opportunities for rentals to be available in larger numbers and greater varieties, with less overhead while still maintaining customer service and customer relationships. Zipcar took the idea of a rental car and saw the opportunity for shorter (one-hour) engagements, all controlled by an app that did everything from book and return the car to function as the key to operate it.

The advent of Citibike, or whatever your community's version is, allows people to use bikes to commute to work, run errands, get to appointments or social engagements, or just sightsee—and then leave the bikes where they land. Fun, affordable, and good for your health and the environment, these bicycles also eliminate the cost factor if you're not in need of—or don't want the hassle of—bike ownership.

Taking the riding conceit further, there is Spin, which offers what, as Dan Winston, former VP of market operations, once said to me, is "the coolest job because I get to think about how to run great scooter businesses, develop great scooter systems in all these different cities, from Kansas City to DC, to Kent State University, to Ann Arbor, Michigan—I get to think about how you do that within the context of different sets of regulations in every place, developing the scalability by working with somebody who is in each city."[1] This is more than simply offering an option for riding a scooter; it's creating the idea of scooter mobility as an option in the first place, which is about changing the consumer's relationship with transportation as a whole. In a place like NYC, there have always been options (car, foot, train, bus, cab), but for the vast majority of the United States, Winston pointed out to me, it is the car or nothing. Shifting the experience from one where cars are seen as the only option to one where the *how* of getting from point A to point B is asked in the first place is part of the mission and success of the company. That is a profound and radical shift in thinking. That there are environmental, health, urban-planning, and other dynamics at play is just part of the narrative that leads to this shift in experience. Some of this is a response to a shifting zeitgeist, but there is also a change that comes inherently when other options arise. And the way to bring people to that new experience is to offer it in a rental form because the commitment level is low. The opportunity for the service provider to show off its prowess in making it easy, fun, and productive to rent something is where the successful organization takes its chance to shine.

Lime, another great example of a rental company, was founded on the simple idea that all communities deserve access to smart, affordable mobility. Through the equitable distribution of shared scooters, bikes, and transit vehicles, it aims to reduce dependence on personal automobiles for short-distance transportation, not to mention create a cleaner, healthier planet.

A CLOSER LOOK: FABULOUS FOR A DAY: RENT THE RUNWAY

Cofounded in 2009 by Harvard Business School classmates Jenn Hyman and Jenny Fleiss, the idea for Rent the Runway emerged when Jenn's sister Becky bought a dress. And not just any dress. As Hyman recounts, the light-bulb moment came during a trip home during her second year of business school. She was sitting in her sister's apartment, where Becky was showing off a dress she planned to wear at a wedding—the cost of which should have been rent for the month! When Hyman tried to offer some sisterly advice—largely, "What about all the great things you already own?"—the response gave birth to the idea that would change how people dress for special occasions. Her sister replied, "My closet is dead to me."[2] What her sister cared about "was the photograph that would exist afterward that would show all of her friends how awesome she looked at the wedding"[3] during a time when social media loomed large and no one wanted to be caught wearing the same outfit twice.

Hyman was struck first, of course, by how much debt her sister was going into. And second, she understood her sister's reasoning. The dress would only be worn once, but the value was in the repeated views and compliments she would receive on social media. Back to Harvard Hyman went, where she reported all of this to Fleiss. Her response? "This sounds fun.

Let's work on this idea together. Who do you think we should call to figure out if it's a good idea?" And Hyman said, "You know, we should really call Diane von Furstenberg." Of course, Hyman didn't actually know Furstenberg, but she was ambitious and creative and figured she could find her email address. Hyman and Fleiss found a number of possible avenues to the woman herself and crafted their message, which ran along the lines of: "Hey, we're two women at Harvard Business School. We have an idea we'd love to come in and talk to you about." And then, as Hyman explains, "this is where luck plays into the situation because she or someone from her office opened that email."

Furstenberg responded, "I'll see you tomorrow at 5 PM."[4]

In the end, she was enormously helpful, even if she was initially skeptical. She advised them not to be designer specific, to get a lot of designers on board from the start. Her feedback, as Hyman said, "gave us permission to make a good, consumer-facing business and to approach the rest of the industry."[5] She also gave the two entrepreneurs some names and numbers, with permission to drop her name to get through to them—among them the president of Neiman Marcus, an HBS alum. His response? "This is a really good idea. Women have been renting the runway from my stores for decades. It's called buying something, keeping the tags on, and then returning it to the store, and it's probably cost me millions." Evidently, it is the dirty little secret of retail, the extraordinarily high rate of returns for dresses and other special-occasion clothing.[6]

Setting up a very successful pop-up shop on the Harvard campus, Hyman and Fleiss realized that they had uncovered a remarkable opportunity.

Rent the Runway took off because it answered questions not everyone realized were being asked. These included the way social media had increased the scrutiny that was previously limited to the famous. Non-VIPs were now posting pictures of themselves on social media regularly enough that repeating outfits had suddenly become something to avoid. People were especially likely to post when decked out in their finest. Worn, posted, and that dress was done.

With multiple generations in mind, an idea took hold. Clothing had always had a shelf life, but it no longer referred to the length of time that something is in fashion. It had become the time in which clothing is seen by those with whom you party as well as those who view the story you post on Instagram. The better the picture, the more fun you appear to be having, the better you look, the more doomed the dress becomes, never to be taken out again. With her Harvard Business School training in her pocket, Hyman set out to break down how to respond to the need she defined. How could she scale enough to make it work?

The first pop-up was in April 2009. At this time, Netflix was mailing DVDs in the mail and Zappos was establishing a trend of trouble-free and no-cost returns. It became clear with some speed that this was an idea with traction. It was what Hyman describes as "the emotional effect. At this pop-up, I saw girls stripping down, trying on these amazing dresses, and feeling beautiful. You saw their facial expressions change, and they threw their shoulders back, and they tousled their hair. And they walked with a new sense of confidence."

But Hyman understood that to deliver something that would make people come back for more, rely on it, and recommend it to others, she had to be able to deliver on the promise that, when you need a dress or outfit, Rent the Runway would have your back. She had to consider depth of inventory and turnaround time for dry cleaning, among other things. (As an interesting side note, and to give a sense of scale, Rent the Runway is the largest user of dry-cleaning services in the country.) All of what she had in mind would require funds right from the get-go; it would only take hold if the depth and breadth of choice and the quality of service delivered was established right from the start. She knew that every time someone turned to Rent the Runway and failed to find what they needed, that was a set of eyes that was unlikely to return at a different time.

Infrastructure was a major consideration. Not only was the issue one of inventory—quantity, size, color—but it was also one of being at just the right place on the fashion curve. Providing the styles that are timeless, that are au courant, and knowing what is around the corner as the next trend—this is a feat best left to professionals. And clients who don't want pieces languishing in their closet after a single wearing are going to be particularly demanding about wanting what they rent to be cutting-edge. But this was another arena in which Hyman excelled.

The other side of the rental coin, especially with something like clothing, is the issue of sustainability. Even if you don't care about the expense of replenishing a closet with the regularity most reserve for groceries, the environment looms large in our collective imaginations. The old way of buying clothing, where you wear something less and less until it one day joins the "giveaway" pile, is antithetical to sustainable thinking. Today, if you don't think about your return on investment ("How many times would I need to wear this dress to justify the cost?"), that's just considered wrong thinking.

Getting Rent the Runway off the ground involved building as long a list of women using it (or likely to use it) as possible. During the summer the *Sex and the City* movie came out in 2008, Hyman and Fleiss set up at the theaters where it was showing, collecting email addresses. As Hyman describes, it was clear that the early days were about rolling up their sleeves and going influencer by influencer. They reached out to friends to spread the word and ask people to join their email list to learn more about their idea. As fate would have it, one of those email addresses was @nytimes .com. The email-address owner turned out to be a twenty-two-year-old technology reporter. They pitched to her their idea for a piece in the business section. The work, the tenacity, the following every line of thinking and opportunity—all of it is both impressive and speaks to why the enterprise worked as well as it did.

That said, it is a business model that would seem extremely vulnerable to an extended period of time when, as recently became reality, no one goes anywhere, people never take off their sweatpants, and the makers of the most comfortable slippers are winning the retail prize. Hyman called her response to the COVID-19 pandemic nothing short of a "second founding." She got her "house in order" as soon as early March 2020, earlier than most and as the reality of the pandemic set in, starting with deep capital cuts and a rigorous examination of every line item of their P&L. Difficult staffing cuts and layoffs had to be done with as much transparency as possible. They asked themselves, "What can we do that our customers need—both right now and down the line?"[7]

The first and biggest shift in thinking came in refocusing the message and purpose of the company to one of sustainability, examining how it could be the source of smart, sustainable fashion. After ten years of working directly with brands, Hyman was in a position to have Rent the Runway continue investing in inventory and allow customers to approach that inventory in one of two ways: renting or buying secondhand. Widely known for building the first "living closet," Hyman expanded the rental parameters, allowing for the old-school one-night or weekend-long rental while also making room for the person who wants to rent clothing for, say, a beach vacation lasting ten days, at the end of which they want to turn over the sundress, cover-up, and floral pedal pushers, none of which they will ever wear as they walk down Madison Avenue.

This shift to include more rental scenarios made for a sustainable, flexible, and responsive company that was ready and waiting when people started to emerge from their homes. It was no longer just about renting that fabulous statement dress for the big event. Now, Rent the Runway is a way to sustainably outfit yourself in a way that has financial and environmental benefits.

The business the founders imagined worked, and not just because it made otherwise unattainable, expensive clothing accessible to those who had the money to spend on it for a limited time. This was a significant part of Hyman's thinking:

> I really think there's a value that women place on self-expression, and clothes make you feel a certain way about yourself. You put on an amazing outfit in the morning, and it makes you feel powerful or beautiful or sexy or relaxed, or however you want to feel that day. There's just a general value in our society right now around individuality and self-expression. And the way that you're going to achieve that with fashion is via variety. And an off-price Forever 21 was as close as many were able to come to it.[8]

The company makes it possible for women to experience the kind of variety previously unavailable to them. They can try something different from what they already know will work—the new, the playful, the irrational, the things you admire in others and wish for yourself. Even if you are going for precisely what you know works, you have the ability to do it with more style, a better cut, a better fit.

Rent the Runway proves the point that "rental" is a word that has many meanings and can accomplish a wide variety of goals. Understanding what your product does and to whom it is aimed and identifying new ways to frame its role in the world is key to staying at the forefront.

A CLOSER LOOK: WASHING THE DISHES IS A FACT OF LIFE NOT EVERYONE EMBRACES THE SAME: WINTERHALTER GERMAN DISHWASHERS

The rental lens can be used to examine even the way appliances are acquired. There is an opportunity for a rental agency to understand, at an elemental level, the value its customers put on a given product. They see customers "struggle to understand what their money buys them to demand accountability rather than accept simple promises,"[9] says Oded Koenigsberg, professor of marketing at the London Business School, whose book, *The Ends Game*, explores different pricing and ownership models.

Metering is one such way of offering accountability and justification for expense, and one example of where it has been used to surprisingly good effect is in the world of German dishwashers. According to a 2018 report by the Council on Contemporary Families, the household chore people hate the most is doing the dishes.[10] The word used to describe the act is "gross." Take that task and imagine it at a larger scale—say, in a hotel or restaurant kitchen—and you've got some very unhappy, soapy hands.

The answer to this detested chore is provided by Winterhalter, a family-owned business started in 1947 that provides dishwashers, racks, detergents, water-treatment supplies, and other services related to cleaning dining ware. These products and services themselves are not so special; what's special is how the company charges customers to clean dishes. It doesn't offer dishwashers by subscription, nor is it a simple rental (take it and pay for the time you have it). Rather, it uses a program called Pay Per Wash. In the spirit of total accountability and cost justification, the program is the ultimate example of "no investment, no risk, and no fixed costs." The interface is simple: the customer logs into the Pay Per Wash portal, enters the number of wash cycles according to specifications previously set, and starts the machines. The charge comes for each completed wash cycle.

The entire process is simple to understand, is simple to execute (with a properly built portal that is stable, reliable, and usable across all known platforms), and puts the economics of the experience in the hands of the customer in a way that breeds loyalty and confidence.

TO BUILD IT SO THEY WILL COME, YOU HAVE TO HAVE EQUIPMENT: UNITED RENTALS

I am not a professional when it comes to repairs and heavyweight outdoor maintenance. And, like so many homeowners, it was only with the experience of a big storm passing through and the attendant damage, cleanup, and other maintenance chores that I got a brief lesson.

In one dramatic storm (it may have been Hurricane Sandy), a tree fell, blocking our driveway. We were literally trapped in our home. When I headed out with my handheld saw, it didn't take me long to realize that my tool did not stand up to the task. Because we were one of many whose newfound arboreal situation required tools we hadn't needed in the past, we had to wait some time before we found someone with a chainsaw to come by and chop up the driveway-blocking trunk.

In my impatience with how long it took and how annoying it was to be beholden to someone else to do what I thought I could do, I thought, *I should buy a chainsaw*. This, despite the fact that I am pretty much as far from a chainsaw-owning kind of guy as they come. But I headed to my local Ace Hardware, and the owner, Joe, showed me the smallest version—a kind of Tonka toy for chainsaws. Tricked out with goggles and heavy gloves, informed as to which gasoline to use for it, and having been taught how to use it without ending up in an ER, I set off home. And it sat, untouched, in my basement for a year. When the next storm came, no one was more excited than I to see that some of my trees had taken a hit. Sadly, I learned the next lesson of chainsaw ownership: if you don't use it for a year, it won't always work when you try to use it again.

The lesson I learned was that I had no business owning a chainsaw. What I really needed was access to a rental company that could provide me with the kind of tools that play such an episodic role in my life that ownership of them is simply nonsensical. My local hardware store didn't rent, and I was keenly aware that when I would next need these tools, I would not be the only one. How to find a reliable source? To assuage my guilt, I keep my chainsaw in top condition, bringing it in for an oil change and cleaning it regularly and regardless of frequency of use. I know that I will never be trapped in my house because of a fallen tree again. But I also recognize how I would rather rent than buy.

This is not a lesson anyone in construction and project management needs to learn. United Rentals is the answer to the question "Who do you turn to when you need the machinery necessary to build bridges, hospitals, apartment buildings, airports, and [fill in your favorite large construction project here]?" A multibillion-dollar company, its focus is broadly supplying what a large project will need. If you are building an airport and need a boom lift or scissor lift (indeed, there is a difference, and I now know what that is), you have the choice of buying one and using it as much as you can—or just renting it from United. A quick survey of many construction sites will yield countless equipment emblazoned with the United logo. When you see it, you know the people overseeing the budget made the decision that renting makes more sense than buying.

The range of services it offers speaks to its understanding of what is best rented: trucks, aerial work platforms, counterbalance forklifts, earth movers, compressors. It covers the needs for equipment used in confined spaces (trench safety), power generators and mobile climate-control units, gear used for moving large quantities of fluids of various kinds, and onsite services like portable toilets and shower trailers. It even offers drone services, if you are so inclined. As its promotional materials state, United Rentals's ambitions are as broad as its products are enormous: "We are committed to: helping our customers become more successful by offering them a modern, diverse, and reliable fleet of equipment for rent or sale, as well as providing outstanding service."

Tony Leopold, senior vice president of strategy, digital, and business development at United Rentals, brought me up to speed on the basics of what drives success and failure in the rental category, starting with economic factors. The higher the cost of a piece of construction equipment and the shorter the time you need it, the more simple the math becomes. Purchase price divided by the amount of time you're going to use it—you will often find it makes more sense to rent rather than buy.

But the issues of availability and accessibility echo my concern that when I want a chainsaw, everyone else will, too. If you only use a car one month out of the year, why pay to own it for the other eleven months, right? But if you won't be able to get what you need when you need it, the economic advantage of renting starts to fade. For United Rentals, if a construction manager needs a piece of equipment, they need exactly that piece of equipment. They need it tomorrow, not next week, because to not have it tomorrow is to hold up an entire step in the construction process, and that affects delivery dates. So, to be successful in the commercial equipment-rental business, you have to have the right equipment, it has to be available relatively quickly, and it must be well maintained so it will reliably function for the entirety of its rental period.

This is what differentiates the good rental agency from the one that you are less likely to return to: understanding how need rises and falls and having the right amount in inventory to guarantee you can be there for your customers when they need you. And, according to Leopold, forward planning is not a hallmark of the industries he serves: "More than half of our volume are people who need something today." That is, to say the least, an extraordinarily high percentage. The preparation on United Rentals's end of things is mind-boggling. Leopold continued, "I would say a lot of our business is short-term in nature. Our customer may know that they need it, but they wait a day before they call you. But, most of the time, it's either today or tomorrow. Sometimes, it's legitimately last minute: 'Hey, my water truck broke.' Or it's something they do own, but it failed or broke down. Sometimes, we step in when someone else's rental fails."[11]

In addition, keeping an eye on other factors—like availability of new products in the supply chain—plays a significant role and requires the kind of industry knowledge and crystal ball–like prescience a longtime professional brings to the party. Leopold told me when we spoke recently,

> I feel like we're in another shift right now. As we speak, the supply-chain constraints that have happened—you can hardly even get new equipment anymore. What happens then is people start to find it anywhere they can. They're going to soak up whatever rental is valuable because the ownership avenue is closed off. We've seen what I'll call the "third leg," which may be temporary because I would expect, over time, the supply chain to normalize. But for now, people have to rely on us. As a result, we're running higher levels of utilization than we've ever had in the history of this company.

The role of a good rental agency, true of this one but applicable when considering others as well, is to be a way to use the newest and the best. I can't always afford what's high-end, just as someone who wants to wear designer clothing can't always afford to buy it outright. But having the chance to rent the newest, best, top of the line—be it dress or transformer—is part of a rental company's allure. In the case of United Rentals, "we refresh our fleets every seven years. This gives us an opportunity to usually have more modern equipment to rent."[12]

The newest, the best, the right type—these are all enormously important to a strong rental service. When two thirds or more of your business caters to same- or next-day needs, having what people need when they need it—reliably and every time they come to you—will be your greatest sales strength. Leopold sees this as one of the key reasons United Rentals dominates an industry where it can be difficult to distinguish yourself.

> What people care about is, "I can trust you to get it to me, right when I need it, right?" The trust factor is big. You have three workers due to show up on a worksite on Monday at 8 AM, but they can only work if the equipment to get the job done is there on Monday at 8 AM. I can say [to them] with all certainty, "I got you, buddy; we're going to be there on time—you can trust me. And if we [aren't], I know I'm going to screw up your day, I'm going to cost you money. If I don't deliver, you won't ever use me again."[13]

United Rentals knows what it can deliver and when it can deliver it, and it makes commitments it intends to keep. When I muse aloud about the famous *Seinfeld* scene in which Jerry and Elaine show up to rent a car, only to find that the word "reservation" is taken pretty lightly (Agent: "Yes, we do [have your reservation]. Unfortunately, we ran out of cars. Jerry: "But the reservation keeps the car here. That's why you have the reservation."),[14] Leopold nods along with me. In his world, when you say it will be there, it will be there—or you will never see those customers again.

One of my favorite Thomas Friedman quotes is his recollection of Larry Summers's words: "No one has ever washed a rented car." He was making the excellent point that when you rent, you don't care about an item's maintenance, except to the extent that it must work for you. The point can be taken even further: when you rent, you give no thought to what it takes for someone to provide that thing or service to you. You just want what you want to be available and ready for you, as promised. Taking the rental route means bringing a deep knowledge of what that means to the customers to whom you seek to rent. Don't confine yourself to the prohibitively expensive or the rarely used. What sustainability and ease of experience has shown us is that consumers know that ownership—all ownership—comes with work and responsibility, not to mention the use of resources. The tide is turning against the trend of ownership; let your company be there to answer the call.

APPROACH THINGS AS A BROKER

You've no doubt heard it said that there are two sides to every story. Two sides to every story is the storyline for this lens of approaching things as a broker. We are going to look at the unique challenges of building and maintaining a successful business with a two-sided market, of which there are several in the experience-disruption category. The easiest way to think about what constitutes a two-sided market is to consider a business that facilitates direct interaction between suppliers and users via an intermediary platform. Among the two most well-known examples are Airbnb, which has to recruit and retain homeowners who want to rent their residences and, on the other side, the people who stay in their homes, and Uber, which has to recruit and retain drivers with cars as well as the people who wish to ride in these cars.

Both sides of each of these businesses pose strategic and executional challenges. This is true no matter how simple the market. My daughter, home from college for the summer, is making extra money as a "Dasher." She sits around our home until her phone buzzes from the DoorDash app. She then walks to a restaurant a block away from our home and delivers a meal to someone who lives a few blocks in the other direction. Without the two-sided app that DoorDash uses, she would never know of the meals that need to be delivered, nor the people who want them.

Remember what Groucho Marx said about how he wouldn't be a member of a club that would have him as a member? The two-sided market depends on those willing to set those insecurities and issues aside and get on board: the influencers and those who follow where they go. It is only by way of a preponderance of people stepping up and joining on both sides that you get the density of participation required to make the service viable.

THE PUSH–PULL OF THE TWO-SIDED MARKET

The two-sided market is a juggling act. You are a brand, which means you need to monitor and be mindful of what is being provided by the supply side and how it is being received by those demanding a good experience on the other. It is a dynamic that is rife with strategic and execution challenges, all while you try to stay profitable. The chicken and the egg are always in flux. In the case of Uber, it's the issue of having the right number of drivers for a given number of people wanting a ride at a particular time. Events, weather, political turmoil, and local rhythms are just a drop in the bucket of what stands in the way of achieving this balance.

Successfully sustaining each side of these businesses poses a uniquely difficult strategic and executional challenge. And, obviously, successfully doing so means staying profitable. It's a chicken-and-egg dilemma.

Chicken-and-egg strategy problems arise when the value proposition to each of two separate groups depends on penetration in the other. An example is an auction site like eBay, with the number of buyers driving attractiveness to sellers, and likewise the number of sellers driving attractiveness to buyers.

Customers—the demanders—want a platform that has a great variety of suppliers, and suppliers will only take part if there is adequate demand. Which comes first? Equally challenging is maintaining quality, especially when many of the suppliers in two-sided markets are independent contractors, be they Airbnb homeowners who rent out their places, Uber drivers who use their own cars, or owners of city garages, who are on the supply side of the parking-space algorithm.

As difficult as the challenge of building a two-sided market may be, some of the most powerful companies in our modern economy were started by marketers who looked through this lens and saw the opportunity to act as a broker and change consumer behavior. Etsy, eBay, Uber, and Airbnb have had a disruptive impact on their respective categories. So, too, have many smaller, but also successful, two-sided marketers.

CHANGING THE WAY WE GET AND STAY PLACES, CHANGING CULTURE

Airbnb and Uber were each launched by entrepreneurs who saw an opportunity to disrupt a specific category. Like many, but not all, of the other examples of experience disruption, these entrepreneurial dreamers did not rely on "making something," requiring the purchase of raw materials, production lines, and distribution channels. Rather, these breakthrough entrepreneurs recognized that you could utilize a platform to create value for two or more user groups (and themselves), connecting those who supply a service with those who use that service—in the case of Airbnb, accommodations while traveling, and in the case of Uber, transportation. The key to success for those that oversee these platforms is the ability to maintain equilibrium between both sides of the market. They must ensure that both sides of their respective businesses are valuable to the respective stakeholders.

Uber started as a simple idea. What if you could request a ride from your phone? What Uber did with that idea—and the effect it's had on daily life and on industries from transport to delivery, to the automotive world, to too many to list here—is inarguable. So, too, is the controversy it has wrought. In search of a taxi on a snowy evening, its founders, Travis Kalanick and Garrett Camp, saw an opportunity to change the way people hail rides, and the rest is history.

There are, as is so often the case, two sides to the Uber story: one that allows us to understand the profound difficulties in doing what they did as well as they did, and one to show how success can exceed expectations. Regarding the former, an enterprise like Uber required not just drivers and passengers but also the right number of drivers at a given time to avoid long wait times, as well as enough demand for drivers in the first place to pay drivers a living wage and to encourage them to keep driving. On the other side of that market, Uber also needed customers who would adopt a new way of doing things (open an app rather than hailing a taxi) in great enough numbers to make the enterprise worthwhile. That balancing act was the technological equivalent of hitting a very difficult maneuver on the gymnastics floor. Height, number of flips in the air, and form—they all had to be just right for everything to click.

Uber is now an international phenomenon that disrupted, transformed, and rewrote how we think of getting from Point A to Point B, so much so that "uber" has become a verb as universal as "google."

What looks like a simple pairing app—driver to rider—is a wildly complicated interface with a global operation behind it. The app is the top layer of what are individual networks of smaller groups representing geographical areas. For each of those areas, the system (drivers and riders) had to be established and scaled. Understanding the supply, demand, and technological infrastructure that brought those two elements together was the job of an organization with an eye on both the big picture and the minutiae, all at the same time.

When you think about an organization's need to pay attention to both sides of an equation in order to add up to the greatest market share, Uber is an ideal example. Each market has a leader, a regional general manager, who is responsible for the balance between rider and driver and what happens between them. They are responsible for revenue and losses in that area, coordinate the operations, and are involved at a granular level with any and all difficulties that might arise in a given place. Within a given area, there are those whose sole mission is to add to and corral the driver pool, recruiting to which is among the most vital activities within the organization. Uber spends an enormous amount on increasing its driver number; quite simply, adding drivers means adding business. No drivers means no business.

Supply and demand is writ large in the world of Uber, as it is in any two-sided market organization. The Uber leaders track each of the markets they serve on a weekly basis with a level of minutiae that is impressive. They track revenue, of course, but they know all the other metrics as well. How much is too much surge pricing, and how many people are canceling because the wait time is too long? Too much surge will send customers to other transport options; too few drivers after a big local event means wait times will also send riders elsewhere. Set too many drivers up during a time when fewer riders are hailing, and you'll lose those drivers to other parts of the gig economy.

Understanding each side with a high level of intimacy and nuance is necessary. For Uber, knowing about the cities where it operates, where the cool neighborhoods are, and when people typically eat dinner in a given region is only a drop in the detail bucket that is the algorithmic world in which it functions. How and when surge pricing is introduced requires Uber to know an enormous amount about a particular city and both its users and drivers. In other words, thinking globally—availing itself of the strength and knowledge that comes with increasing global success—and keeping boots on the ground in each of its specific markets necessitates a hyper-local understanding of what is needed and how it is best provided.

Uber brought the concept of acting as the broker to a new place and, in doing so, not only changed its own market but also showed the ways in which a third-party entity can disrupt and realign a whole host of markets. It examined, understood, and stayed on top of all the elements at play; saw the ways in which it needed to adjust its own model to fit the various regions and countries in which it worked; and established a template for dos and don'ts that will be around far longer than any one company will.

A CLOSER LOOK: MATCHMAKER, MATCHMAKER, MAKE ME A MATCH: ONLINE DATING

Old-school dating was like a song out of Broadway musical *Fiddler on the Roof* ("Matchmaker, matchmaker, make me a match . . .") and has evolved to a place where AI-generated matches are accepted as the norm. In between, there were a lot of iterations, and I had my own. Back when I had been single for a long, long time, my friends decided to help me out. We were all in marketing and advertising, and they decided to bring a marketing-driven approach to solve my single-guy problem. For one of my birthdays, they got together and wrote a positioning statement of different ways they could serve me up to the marketplace. Then they created three ads; of them, the one with the headline "Adventuresome Ad

Executive" was deemed the winner. Then they made an immediate plan and placed the ad in *New York Magazine*, which had a classified section of personal ads. They reviewed the 110 responses and selected eight they thought would make a good match for me. Then they called five of them to do a pre-interview. Finally, on my birthday, they presented three recommended dates. In the name of giving my friends full credit for a gift incredibly well executed, their ribbon on the gift was making restaurant reservations and suggesting conversation topics—but, sadly, they did not provide an AmEx number to cover the cost of drinks with the "finalists." The dates were, ultimately, for naught, but the sentiment and the spirit were noted and appreciated.

Where once meeting online was something people kept quiet about, times have indeed changed. As Guy Raz told me when we spoke, "Today, every young person I know uses a dating app. Every person I know who's single uses a dating app; if you don't use dating apps, you're an oddball. Tinder, Bumble—these products fundamentally changed how people behave around connecting." My unscientific survey suggests that not only is this true, but it is also true of single people in every generation.

Bringing people together online when they would otherwise have no reason to run into one another is as interesting as it is tricky. For this and so many other reasons, it's never been easy to find a partner. But the modern practice of looking online for a mate (or just company for some period of time—no judgments) became even more firmly entrenched in such a time when the pandemic made us all stay home and stream rather than hit the town and make new friends. The number of popular dating apps and sites that can help you make connections that lead to a long-term relationship, or even a fun fling, are many, and the approaches they take are wildly varied. Thanks to the creative minds who are always thinking about fine-tuning (or taking a big leap into the new) ways a person might want to find someone, self-identified groups of people congregate on different apps depending on what they want, who they are looking for, and what criteria they bring to their search.

Tinder started as the hookup app and continues to serve that population, but it became so ubiquitous that now everyone goes to Tinder: looking for friends, a one-nighter, or longer-term relationships. But the app remains quippy and brief in its presentation, almost entirely dependent on flicking right and left, moving quickly, working the numbers game. On Hinge, the idea is to find people you may not know personally but who have a degree or three of connection to you. You offer access to your social media, and Hinge finds people who know people that know you.

Bumble took the bold step of shifting the retro dynamics so often employed online that see men doing most of the initial contacting—and often doing so in creepy or unwelcome ways. Bumble's hook was to be the dating platform where women are in control. On Bumble, men can't contact women; women have to make the first move. Just this simple shift in how the two-sided market works makes the same people, cutting and pasting the same bits of biographical information into each of their profiles, feel significantly different. How? The experience is different. It is different when you are in an app where you know you will never find inappropriate pictures of a man you've never met waiting for you.

On Coffee Meets Bagel, the clock starts ticking as soon as you start communicating, which pushes both parties to step up and speak/write before the seven-day chat window ends, addressing the long lag time that so often plagues in-app communication between the matched.

Each platform offers its own tweak to the approach and language of introducing people to others they don't know in the hope of a satisfying—whatever that may mean for you—end. All of them rely on large numbers of people to step up and participate. Drawing them in and keeping them there and active, while doing enough to keep everyone safe and accountable, is no small feat.

Arizona State University assistant professor Liesel Sharabi, who works out of the school's Relationships and Technology Lab, does research that focuses on the connection between communication technologies and interpersonal relationships. She brings some perspective to and makes some interesting observations about the dating ecosystem that has developed over time. First, she makes the point that "old-school" dating no longer refers to meeting at work, at the local watering hole, or via friends introducing friends. The old way harkens back to the more recent but still vestigial sound of the AOL dial-up, with Meg Ryan and Tom Hanks pecking away at their respective keyboards in 1998's *You've Got Mail*. While the romance depicted there feels as far away from today's world as any, the role it played cannot be undersold. "*You've Got Mail* was important for bringing online relationships into the mainstream,"[1] Sharabi notes. Once online dating came out of the shadows, as it were, the disruption to what was considered a "normal" way to meet a romantic partner was thoroughly established. The experience transformed.

Who knows what the future holds for online or virtual dating experiences? Dr. Samantha Sterling, chief strategy officer at AKQA, shared some thinking as to where all of this might be heading. She sees one potential direction in virtual-dating meetups. Just as Peloton puts the real-life trainer in your screen or how MIRROR brings its trainer to you in a full-length wall mirror—allowing that person to pump you up, direct your workout, and otherwise be with you without, you know, being with you—Sterling sees a similar system as a potential way to meet matches. "This could be the future of dating. At the moment, we tend to be limited to photos, and some dating apps are slow to move into video. But the idea that these fitness mirrors could actually be the technology which can spill into dating—I think it's quite an interesting idea."[2]

Certainly, her theories are borne out in the way online dating responded to the pandemic. As virtual as online dating is, it does depend on eventually meeting in person. In fact, many apps do everything in their power to prompt people to put down the phone and physically meet the person they've been connecting with virtually: connections expire, time limits are put on chat windows, etc. But when people cannot leave their homes and, more to the point, people are explicitly asked to remain in their immediate bubble of acquaintances, onboarding a new person into your life becomes far more difficult. The apps responded; they made use of virtual video options and tried to make it possible for those first dates to happen in the virtual world. Like many media-streaming apps (which introduced ways to "watch together" from our respective homes), they tried to be creative. They offered ways that made the event more than just clicking a button and going face-to-face with a perfect stranger with whom you've exchanged only some (or many) messages. Without the background din of a restaurant or the foliage and birdsong of a preliminary walk, the minutes can tick by rather slowly. The apps tried to fill that space, making use of the technology available to create a customer experience that supported the reality in which we were living, and made it possible for their users to take those early steps toward making a new acquaintance.

With these kinds of apps, you're not just putting folks together; you are responsible for their experience. In each of these scenarios, there are people and things that are in need of a bridge, whether they know it or not. The creativity behind how that bridge is developed, the ease with which the participants can access and cross the bridge, and how well the broker can control and deliver a quality product to both sides—this is where the magic lies.

A CLOSER LOOK: MATCH A SOFA, ROOM, HOUSE, OR EXPERIENCE WITH THE GUEST WHO WANTS OR NEEDS IT: AIRBNB

Airbnb is the quintessential Silicon Valley story. Two former classmates, Brian Chesky and Joe Gebbia, found and solved an unfulfilled need in the market. Their idea for Airbnb was to offer a different experience from that of hotels, one where the guest can choose lodging that appeals to them. And it stands in perfect opposition to what hotels promoted about themselves for so long. In the *Mad Men* days, the beauty of staying at, say, a Hilton was that you knew exactly what it would be—where the lobby store was located, if ice machines were on every floor or every other floor, how the check-in process worked, and what the room would look like and provide. As fictional advertising icon Don Draper said in his pitch to Hilton, "Now there's one word that promises the thrill of international travel with the comfort of home—Hilton. How do you say 'ice water' in Italian? 'Hilton.' How do you say 'hamburger' in Japanese? 'Hilton.' Hilton—it's the same in every language."[3] But the tide has turned since then, and now no one wants the usual. People want something different—an *experience*—and they want something where they control the metrics: choosing a private house or a room in a house; pool, yes or no; pets allowed or not; etc.

That said, as Raz mentioned, the success of Airbnb does not spell the doom of hotels. "I think there's still very strong reasons why, if you're on a family vacation, why you would want to go to a Four Seasons resort or a Marriott resort. Airbnb certainly can't compete with that. They're never going to put those places out of business, and there'll always be a place for those companies. But I think how people travel now and how they seek out accommodation includes an option that just didn't exist in any form or fashion a short time ago."[4]

Chesky and Gebbia launched the service out of a loft apartment in San Francisco and, within five years, by mid-2013 had nine million customers. Urban legend has it that the loft became so crowded with employees that the founders left and rented an Airbnb apartment nearby. It's important to think about how basic the premise was, especially to the extent that it required no new technology. It was a website, one on which someone could go to find an alternative to a hotel. They unlocked the personal market, looking at what was there all along with new eyes. Why couldn't staying on someone's couch or in an extra bedroom or booking the whole residence, they asked, all be options?

What we consider normal today was actually an odd proposition in the not-so-distant past. Airbnb's founders overcame people asking why you would want to stay in a stranger's house instead of a reliably consistent hotel. They overcame the initial resistance to having perfect strangers stay in your home. What is perfectly normal now felt, at the beginning, weird. To a great extent, they turned the lodging experience on its ear and asked, "What if it were never the same way twice? How cool is that?"

Because every home is different, they went to market with thousands and thousands of unique experiences, each one an authentic and potential story to share on social media, all tailor-made for a variety of audiences. By the time the pandemic rolled around, when hotels were closed or considered unwise, Airbnb provided experiences that were the salvation for many. You could hop onto the website and decide where you wanted to be. If you wanted a true chef's kitchen or a house with lots of musical instruments you were allowed to use—there was simply no end to the kinds of experiences available.

The beauty of the dynamic between Airbnb, host, and guest is the extent to which both Airbnb and the host are offered clear views of what people want, how they want it, and when they want it, with a big helping of all the stuff they hate. There is a vast amount of data generated every day, and

Airbnb has the computing power to process it. It makes for better listings and adaptable support for the platform for the hosts as well as the guests.

The initial seismic shift in behavior inspired by Airbnb made people think of Airbnb first instead of a hotel when they thought of travel. This shift, of course, relied and continues to rely on the broker relationship remaining tightly bound to the ethos of Airbnb, with hosts doing all they can to make for a great stay.

One of the bigger challenges to playing the role of broker is that you can only control what you control—the platform, the website, the app, how the data is collected, and how the data is used to generate suggestions and matches for guests. The hosts, however, are the wild card. Determining how to support, guide, prod, and cajole hosts to do Airbnb proud and be the kind of host that generates repeat users of Airbnb is a significant part of the broker relationship. Airbnb guidance for hosts abounds on the internet:

> When a guest books an Airbnb, hosts can ask simple questions like "What is the purpose of your stay?" Asking this is a great way to gain valuable information from your guest that you could use to personalize their stay and, therefore, make it more memorable. Maybe they are on a getaway, traveling with a friend, or even on their honeymoon. You take advantage of this information to prepare a welcome basket, recommendation book/binder, and perhaps even your decorations. These are small items that you can put together that can significantly impact the guest experience.
>
> While it may take a little more effort to make a welcome basket or a recommendation book for your guests, the result is worth your time. You create a more memorable experience for your guest and a better review for the host (a win-win for both parties) . . . There are endless ways to make your guest feel welcome, and these are only the start of what you can do for your guest. Be creative with

the information that your guest provides and make it the Airbnb experience they would remember.[5]

These guidelines may feel like Hosting 101, but they are only the beginning of what needs to exist for a broker to rely on providers who are not in their employ. Returning to the 101 side of things, one of the initial bits of advice they offer: an essential part of a great guest experience is with a clean Airbnb. There is even a third-party service called TurnoverBnB for those hosts unable or unwilling to do what is necessary to offer a clean spot but willing to pay for the privilege of not partaking.

A CLOSER LOOK: ONE-STOP INSURANCE WITH AN INFORMATION-RICH BROKER: POLICYGENIUS

When I hear the words "insurance agent," my mind (like that of many others, I suspect) turns to 1993's *Groundhog Day* and its infamously annoying high-school-classmate-turned-insurance-agent, Ned Ryerson. He pesters Bill Murray's character relentlessly and delivers one of my favorite lines:

> I have not seen this guy for twenty years. He comes up to me, and then he buys whole life, term, uniflex, fire, theft, auto, dental, health, with the optional death and dismemberment plan, water damage . . . Phil, this is the best day of my life.[6]

All joking aside, selling insurance is incredibly difficult. To do it successfully, you have to be really good. There's a reason why there is a very high attrition rate among insurance salespeople—selling insurance is really hard to do. And the reason that it's hard to do, as the cofounder of

Policygenius, Jennifer Fitzgerald, explains, is that insurance is difficult to shop for.

> You want to buy a pair of shoes. You go to the place where you buy shoes, and you pick a pair that you like, and you know how to do that because you do it all the time, right? You go to Expedia, or you go to one of the other flight aggregators, you look at prices checking source A and source B, then you pick the cheapest one. We all have our routines for this. People don't know how to buy insurance. People don't know how to shop for insurance. People have no idea what are the different types of life insurance, for example, and what's right for them. So we knew that great content and content that doesn't read like it's written by underwriters was going to be a big part of our brand.[7]

You can offer someone a pair of sneakers and ask them to walk around the room, bounce up and down, and do a little dance. If they don't like what they buy, they can return it. The younger you are, the more likely it is that you are used to most of your purchases being for something tangible. Insurance is the ultimate intangible. It's a concept that is difficult to explain and even harder to make relevant to younger audiences. As an intangible, it is harder to sell, and it is even harder to prove your trustworthiness when you're selling it.

Policygenius has control that others in the role of agent do not have. It can determine which policies are solid, offered by reliable sources, and pass muster in ways that allow it to join such policies together. Insurance agents establish trust by offering good information about the best companies with a user interface that makes it easy to do what you need to do. When Policygenius presents the insurance options, it appears more agnostic, especially when compared to an agent who always seems to be pushing for one policy over another for reasons that may or may not be commission-based.

Using virtual tools to provide an education on a topic about which most enter knowing little or nothing is a key part of what Policygenius understood was necessary and what it now does so well. Information is good, and information provided in a way that makes the user interface with that information effective and accessible is the goal. Often, Fitzgerald has found, first-time insurance buyers arrive at their door because a trigger of some kind has occurred in their lives. "The biggest trigger for life insurance is having a child, is what we have found in our consumer research. Specifically, it's having child number two because when people have their first child, they're so overwhelmed by being a parent, that's all they can think about. So, they actually don't get around to the life insurance until they have child number two, or when child number one is old enough that they start to think about life insurance or homeowners insurance."[8]

Insurance is the opposite of most online purchases. It is not an impulse purchase. It is a multistep journey. As Fitzgerald says,

Insurance, as you probably know—it's a very considered purchase. You don't wake up one morning saying, "Great, today I'm gonna get life insurance. And I know exactly what I want, how much I want, and where to go." It's a pretty long decision journey. There's lots of research involved because nobody's an expert on insurance, right? Even very financially savvy consumers don't know a lot about insurance. So we knew that a key part of our value proposition and a key part to our success was making sure that we had the right content and the right tools along every step of that journey.[9]

Personally, I have been fortunate in my career to have worked with many insurance companies, from MetLife to New York Life to AIG, and many others. As Fitzgerald has put it so well, there are so many reasons why insurance can be a tricky sell to the younger market. You can't touch it, you can't try it on or drive it around the block, and it's there to address an intangible future problem. Selling the intangible is always a challenge, and this is exacerbated when you try to sell it to a generation that feeds on tangibility and wants instant gratification. And if they're lucky, consumers will never even use the insurance product, whether they are protecting their car, house, or life.

The next challenge is the stigma attached to insurance, in that it is an industry thought to be inherently untrustworthy. This often means that you have to push really hard to sell it, but when you are pushing a sale, you can sound insincere.

What Policygenius does so well is lay out a lot of information, make it clear what its relationship is to the plans it sells, and make clear the metrics it uses to offer information about the policies it lists. It's just as hard to buy insurance as it is to sell it. But if the information isn't presented in just the right way, with absolute clarity and with an ease of comparison, you'll lose your audience.

Fitzgerald has laser vision when it comes to the challenges of selling insurance and the obstacles that Policygenius sets out to overcome.

It's not straightforward how to buy and make that purchasing decision. Are you optimizing for price? How does price work? How does price work across the different flavors of life insurance? How do you choose between Prudential and Lincoln, Financial and MetLife? In every single dimension you can think of, insurance is different than buying a flight. And it's also high stakes, right? If you get life insurance wrong, your family will eventually face the worst-case scenario. If you, the breadwinner in your household, dies prematurely, and it turns out you didn't buy the right life insurance, or you didn't buy enough life insurance, that's a decision with serious ramifications. Same thing with homeowners insurance, right? House floods. Whoops. You didn't know that home insurance didn't cover floods. This is such a high-consideration, high-stakes decision.[10]

And this is why Fitzgerald balks at comparisons between what she does at Policygenius and something like, say, Expedia. She is not the Kayak of insurance. She sees these types of comparisons as an oversimplification of what makes doing what they do well so hard to do well. Travel bookings are, by definition, a "high-frequency purchase. It's low stakes; if you get it wrong, no big deal. You may end up paying a little bit more than you should have. And it's something that you know how to do because you do it so often. Buying insurance, it's the exact opposite in every dimension. You don't do it that often with life insurance—you may buy it, at most, two to three times over your life."[11]

This is why Policygenius focuses so much of its efforts on the reliability and trustworthy factor, building trust and offering information that is a solid guide to a confusing category. And because it comes in the form that it does, it frames itself in a way that makes itself intelligible for first-time buyers, the younger generation. And let's face it: many young people (read: millennials) prefer to interact via text or app instead of with face-to-face communication. They are used to doing everything online and not meeting with many people. They don't go to stores, they double-click; they don't order at restaurants, they use Grubhub or UberEats. As a result, they interact with, and probably trust, salespeople less. They probably trust salespeople even less than my generation trusted the poor salespeople portrayed by Ned Ryerson. So the first task to be able to sell something as difficult as insurance to a consumer is to build trust.

As millenials age—nearing the age at which insurance policies are relevant, necessary, or, at least, a good idea—they are proving to be an incredibly tough population to break through to. In other words, insurance sales are getting harder and harder as these generations defined by different forms of communication age into ones that need these kinds of services.

Policygenius understands that the young person who understands the need for and importance of buying insurance does not, in any shape or form, want to deal with a human being when they do so. The last thing they want is a person applying powers of persuasion. If they have questions, they want the ability to chat online with a person who can answer the question they have and then leave them be. They want to be left to flip around, read a bit, respond to a text, watch something, read Reddit, then circle back to consider insurance; in other words, they want to multitask their research experience.

Having established trust, the two-sided broker business of Policygenius was established. The goal was not to offer a comprehensive look at every kind of policy available. Instead, it narrows options to a manageable number. It helps you make decisions that are informed but fast. It doesn't try to spend hours with you, helping you understand the market—it just wants to sell you what you need as quickly as possible. This makes Policygenius the poster child for how important communication is in the two-sided market. Clearly state your offer, explain the benefits of your offer, and then show why the options you are presenting are all quality—and then it's up to the customer to make a decision based on the information provided. But, and this cannot be stated enough, customers have to trust the quality of your information and that the product will work as promised. Fitzgerald knew it would take a long time to become the trusted adviser online, providing content that would resonate with younger consumers, but focusing on communication helped Policygenius achieve that.

A CLOSER LOOK: AUTHENTICITY AND FOOD COME TOGETHER IN YOUR HOME: SHEF AND WOODSPOON

What if you had a lot of friends from all over the world who were incredible cooks? And let's say they took turns delivering meals to you that were both delicious and chosen with your particular tastes, allergies, and other predilections in mind. You would probably be pretty excited.

Younger generations tend to be passionate about authenticity. They bring a lot of critical thinking when they approach a brand or buying decision, and a critical component is the answer to the questions: Is this authentic? Is it real? Is it different? And, also important, what is the story behind it? Does it have purpose? Does it have a meaning that goes beyond the product or experience, one that I would want to share with other people? For many, having an experience interesting enough to share about is a part of why they do it in the first place. The story to be shared with their friends must have many dimensions. Food carries such stories.

Shef and WoodSpoon are two different brokered, two-sided markets with a similar structure and offering. Both are based in New York City. Both offer customers a range of offerings, prepared by local cooks who have featured biographies and other ways to personalize the experience. The delivery is always refrigerated, and both websites stipulate the steps they take to guarantee the safety of the food their various chefs prepare.

Both embody the idea of bringing an eclectic and international group of cooks together for your dining pleasure and an experience that promises authenticity and difference of a shareable quality. They both offer entry to a pool of cooks you would never otherwise encounter, cooks who make foods that may or may not be familiar to you, and deliver these homemade meals to your home.

Authenticity, of course, is what's key. When you order a meal from a real Afghan cook or a real Turkish cook, it goes beyond what even visiting a particular restaurant might provide. What these two websites do is as simple as they are quite remarkable. The idea behind brokering these particular talents to a customer base that is New York City's food-curious speaks perfectly to the times in every sense. The strength of the authenticity on the one side and the conviction that the real, the different, the shareable is worth the effort of finding it on the other is clear.

Both of these companies function as brokers for individual cooks who would otherwise never have the resources to market and spread the word about their cooking and for customers who get the chance to try food they otherwise would not have access to. Ordering food from one of these websites supports local cooks and lets people explore other cultures, and it all comes in a form that you just heat and eat.

The structure of the websites speaks to the light touch of the people behind them. While the branding is clear—WoodSpoon and Shef are the voices you hear—the individual cooks can link to themselves, control what is said about them and their food, and otherwise show real agency in putting themselves forward. And because there is a vetting process that considers health as well as quality, customers can have expectations, and the broker—WoodSpoon or Shef—can control enough to stand behind what it offers.

Brokering of any kind means understanding the kinds of liability a dynamic or situation might create. In this combination of purpose and authenticity that drives both Shef and WoodSpoon, there are a lot of hoops to navigate, regarding kitchen, sanitation, and health guidelines, all of which were mostly designed for restaurants in order to avoid, basically, making anyone sick. An excellent intent, of course, but when rules created for mass-produced meals in an industrial kitchen, run by large numbers of people, get applied to a woman standing in her kitchen in Queens, it might be time for rules to get adapted. So these companies must attend to these things to support both sides of their market.

These are the early days of both of these two-sided markets, but the initial signs are excellent. As of early 2022, WoodSpoon has seen an average monthly growth of its customer base of 17 percent and an average monthly growth of home chefs on the platform of 25 percent. Currently, WoodSpoon has over three hundred home chefs in its network based in NYC alone. In August, WoodSpoon completed a Series A funding round at $14 million, and in December, WoodSpoon also announced its new catering service to provide companies and their employees with catered home-cooked meal options. WoodSpoon plans to grow its number of employees and further develop the platform as it continues to expand into other major cities across the United States.[12]

While still young, Shef and WoodSpoon are good examples of how looking through this lens of brokering offers tremendous opportunities to find ways of creating new market spaces. Their challenges also speak to the those faced by anyone trying to break new ground. When the world's rules are written for one set of circumstances, it can be hard to squeeze in a new way of doing things without getting shut down. But, as we have seen in so many of these companies, stepping up and creating two-sided markets that bring heretofore unconnected groups together can rewrite the rules of a given industry and give rise to enormous potential.

Taking on the mantle of broker requires the ability to identify strong players on one side and truly know what is wanted or needed by consumers on the other. Your ability to discern, deliver, and maintain a consistent level of service will allow you to deliver an experience only you can provide.

The easy part is knowing that there are drivers with cars and people who need a ride somewhere. Just as any proficient juggler will tell you, a small number of balls are easily kept in the air. Three drivers, three riders—done and done. With a little practice, all six balls are smoothly kept in the air. The challenge is maintaining a balanced supply and demand. It is making sure the experience offered by the supplier is good enough to attract and keep the customer. When two-sided markets fail, they do so not because the opportunity wasn't there; they fail because the broker couldn't keep all the balls in the air. They fail when suppliers fail to materialize or fail to deliver at the promised level of service; they fail when the broker doesn't grasp consumer demand sufficiently to keep the suppliers happily on tap.

When the balance is struck, it must be maintained, and that requires vigilance, yes—but more than that, it requires a broker who understands all of the players and brings an empathy toward and profound appreciation of the issues facing each side.

EXPLORE VIRTUAL OPTIONS

Over the years, I've had the opportunity to go to the Consumer Electronics Show (CES) in Vegas. It's one of my favorite trade shows because it has all the new electronic toys that are about to come onto the market. You can see them, learn about them, and often touch and feel them before they reach prime time. It really doesn't get more fun than this. I use the CES as an opportunity to get out of my professional bubble, but it's also a way to indulge what is a personal interest in the cool tricks and toys that emerge from this industry.

Several years ago, virtual reality started to pop up in places that ran the gamut. At first it was niche, and then it was mainstream. I remember the first time I put on a VR headset. It belonged to a company that was showing how virtual reality could be used to sell aircraft interiors. With the help of the tech, I boarded a large plane, walking onto it as if I were a passenger. I could see the entryway, the lighting, the luggage bins, the seats, the galley. I was able to walk around the inside of the plane. I was able to experience the details of what was being sold in a way no video or photograph could offer.

Since then, VR has only gotten better. A few years back, when I was working with the Marriott hospitality company, it was piloting the use of virtual reality. Team members set up a booth outside of New York City's City Hall, where one hundred couples a day are married. They offered each of the newlyweds the opportunity to step into their virtual-reality booth, where they could tour any Marriott resort around the world. They could see phenomenal settings, services, and comfort offered by each of the properties. It was an incredible sales moment and a terrific use of the technology. It was also a sign of what virtual reality could mean to the travel industry as a whole.

The larger point I'm making here is that in order to understand where the category is going, you have to look at what is available at the cutting edge of technology. Technology will always become more accessible, cheaper, and easier to use; a lot of it will likely land on your iPhone.

There is no doubt that technology allows us to do many things in a virtual space that we used to do face-to-face. We've all experienced it, and it is likely to continue to have a profound effect on how we do things in the future. What will be interesting to note and/or attempt to control will be what reverts back to more traditional methods and what remains in the virtual realm.

When shifting to or adding a virtual dimension to your product or service, think first about to what extent the experience can be enlivened, improved, and defined by you.

The perceptive people who have looked through this lens have identified viable opportunities to build fascinating virtual businesses in categories where the virtual previously never played a part. Be it looking at real estate or exercising, holding meetings or getting math help from a tutor, talking to the pediatrician or getting help with our taxes, the spectrum of disruptive innovation categories is wide and only getting wider.

Going virtual isn't always the boon that it is for so many. During the pandemic, people stopped leaving their homes, and when they did leave, they went to known spaces for finite amounts of time. It made things hard for the real-estate market, which relies so much on the immediate, in-person, and tactile experience that is being in the space you might soon call home. Zillow developed an extensive and sophisticated 3D walk-through experience on its website that was designed to entice those who could not physically trod the floorboards of its listings to feel that they knew the listing well enough to decide whether or not they wanted to live there.

Unfortunately, it was a flop. Well, it failed as a sales (and rental) mechanism, anyway. People simply did not want to buy or rent a place without physically visiting it. The virtual could not replace the corporeal. But the views logged were tremendous. Turns out, looking at real-estate videos is something a lot of people like to do as a hobby, whether they plan to purchase a home or not. And the viewer numbers on Zillow's site were so astronomical, they inspired an SNL skit in which viewing apartments was likened to calling a phone sex line.

THE COVID-19 PANDEMIC FORCED ALL OF US ONLINE

Life during the pandemic was largely lived online. Video calls took over everything from meetings to yoga classes to remote-learning subjects ranging from cooking to math to a foreign language. We got used to having people we'd never met pick out and deliver our groceries. Food outlets of every sort diversified their offerings and services. We learned the importance of new skill training in systems and software. We learned to appreciate game night with the family. Amidst the very real and very distressing challenges the pandemic posed, businesses were forced to see opportunities for creativity, adaptability, and innovation, many of them previously unimagined. Many of these businesses continue to exist—and flourish—as the crescendo of those difficult days pass and we all seek to find the horizon that is the new normal.

The questions that remain are many. Will remote working remain a viable option? Will we continue to order anything and everything online forever? Will we ever return to formal office wear, or will the office become a space in which athleisure is welcome? It is, clearly, anybody's guess. But the opportunity to do things differently that necessity afforded us opens a door for those strategizing beyond the immediate pandemic-ish state in which we live. We now see the new way of doing things and are no longer bound by vestigial ideas of what is "supposed" to be in person versus virtual. There are long-term benefits, ranging from sustainability, overhead, and access considerations, that make the virtual a vital part of any healthy business plan.

A CLOSER LOOK: TEACHING VIRTUALLY IS HARDER THAN IT LOOKS: STANFORD

One of the great pleasures of my life is when I am asked to be a guest speaker for students in an MBA program and can talk to them about branding and marketing. During the pandemic, these talks became virtual. I thought it would be a relatively easy thing to do. I'd take my PowerPoint deck and pop it on Zoom, and the students would see it and my postage stamp–sized head as I spoke, and all would be well.

It was harder than that. First of all, when you teach over Zoom, you're talking into a void. You have few reactions to bounce off of, no body language, very little sound, no ability to "read the room." This means I had no idea if I was boring the pants off of everyone; for all I knew, everyone in the class was online shopping and otherwise doing anything but listening to me. It was a one-way experience. There was no connection with the people to whom I was speaking.

So I was intrigued when, about a year into the pandemic, I read about a Stanford team that had started thinking about this challenge a long time ago and had made some progress well before the pandemic was a twinkle in anyone's eye. Their basic premise was that, in order to engage, you have to make the students larger than a postage stamp on the screen. And, equally important, the sound quality needed to be improved. Curious, I spoke with Bob Smith about his work in developing the necessary technology.

Smith is the director of classroom innovation at Stanford University and was involved with a multiyear-long project aiming to improve class-rooms on campus. The first point he made to me was rather key:

> We have generationally disparate customers. We have to keep in mind, there's the faculty who tend to be—well, they are older. And then there are students, who are not only younger; they've got a different set of expectations, or, at least, are forming sets of expectations about what the space should be like. There's a similar distance between the people who are actually doing the work and people who are the recipients of it, just in terms of years of experi-ence, expectations, familiarity, that sort of thing.[1]

I learned about his work while reading an article that showed a pro-fessor teaching a class on Zoom. Instead of sitting in front of a desktop computer, however, the professor was in an empty lecture hall. He had four large-screen TVs displaying students with almost-normal head sizes. He could walk around and interact with the students because he could look at them by way of the multiple-camera setup rather than into the camera of his computer.[2]

The piece described the challenges of having a meaningful experience of engagement when you have 250 people joining a single event on-screen. The traditional Zoom or Zoom-like setup renders the speaker a unilateral voice speaking into the void. But what if that speaker were speaking to a wall of monitors that replicated the audience of a lecture? What if students that were almost life-size were stacked, much as they would be in the hall, behaving as they did when they used to arrive in person—some actively engaged and staring into the camera, some hunched and scratching away in their notes, and others staring off into space or otherwise making clear that their presence is in physical form only? In this way, a lecturer can tell when material is making sense with the nodding of heads and the "aha" expressions. They can see when a joking aside lands (or doesn't) and can adjust their tempo or tone from a read of the room that approximates a live classroom experience.

What Smith developed was an approach that used the virtual we all know, to some extent, and expanded on it to allow the virtual to be even more effective, to add more to the lives of those using it. Even more, Stanford has modified its lecture halls to make them more virtual-friendly by applying these new approaches to remote-learning setups.

Beyond providing the visual that is so necessary to communication that has some reciprocity, the Stanford setup emphasized the audio in a way that is key but, forgive the pun, largely unsung. Taking a page from the theater, audio's role became front and center. The flat echoes of tone that come with an unassisted audio setup can make a ninety-minute lecture a soporific exercise. Add depth and quality to the sound, and the human voice, with all of its range and emotion, comes alive. The issue of the slight delay that occurs and renders a so-called live interaction rife with the minute delays that interrupt a flow of information, the feeling of true communication, the classroom dynamic truly needs. Smith became quite animated describing the effects: "This is the first time anyone had solved the audio problem, which is that the software, just kind of by itself, made the management of echo canceling and all that invisible and reliable and robust."[3] When an audio setup allows you to walk around and speak with a physicality that is the norm when everyone is in the room together, you get a better-quality sound from the person speaking, and the audience gains the benefit of a voice that is engaged. With cameras set up to catch multiple angles and a person who is roaming more widely than is typically allowed, combined with a more sophisticated audio setup, you have teaching that is far more likely to engage with the material and the students.

The lesson here, as it were, is that we went so quickly from using some virtual tools to relying on them almost exclusively. And we all know this will never go away entirely. The visual, sound, and lighting issues will remain because we will never assume that virtual options are entirely out of the picture ever again. Learning to present information in an engaging way, when it is doomed to be more one-sided than not, has always been a challenge. It is the difference between a gifted lecturer and one who is, shall we say, less so.

The Stanford effort shows an attention to what the news and documentary filmmakers have long known. People have been conveying facts and figures and analysis for decades, to different effect. The shows or films that succeed are those that identify the topics that capture imaginations (of course), but then present them in a way that is dynamic and engaging despite the one-sided nature of the communication.

This is the lesson Stanford took and applied. And it is one that any of us who hope to convey our excitement about a new product or idea must keep in mind. It is never enough to simply convert to the new way, whatever that is. We must engage with the new technology and find ways to make our words richer and more engaging and speak more directly to our customers.

A CLOSER LOOK: A WORKOUT IS VIRTUALLY THE SAME OR BETTER WITH VIRTUAL SUPPORT: VIRTUAL FITNESS

I'm one of those lucky New Yorkers who lives near Central Park. And for many years, I've had the privilege of starting most mornings with a little run in the park around the reservoir. In the early days, I used to put on my sneakers and pop on a Walkman or a radio and listen to music as I ran. In later days, my running experience changed when Nike partnered with Apple and created the Nike Run Club, an app you could download on your iPod and early smartphone.

Instead of just playing music while you ran, you could buy a pair of sneakers that had a little chip in the sole. And that chip would enable your smartphone, one that wasn't nearly as smart as the ones we have today, to know how fast and how far you were going. As a member of the Nike Run Club, you could get support and encouragement, and you could reach out to others for help in reaching goals. Running with a digital personal trainer that knew exactly how well you were doing meant you could receive feedback during your runs. It allowed you to pick the right music you wanted as well as keep track of how you were doing cumulatively. It was a mildly virtual experience that doesn't really hold a candle to the virtual trainers, Pelotons, and MIRRORs of today.

By today's standards, the early version of the Nike Run Club wasn't high tech, but the fact that it offered camaraderie, goal setting, and other trainer-like services, all with a chip in a shoe, was pretty impressive.

What a Difference a Pandemic Makes

Several years back, in pre-pandemic times, a friend of mine joined a startup offering virtual training on people's smartphones. His pitch to me was "Allen, how much are you currently paying Equinox, your gym, for a training session?" I told him the amount—and, of course, he told me I was crazy. "You can use this virtual training instead, and you'll get it for one fourth the price with a better trainer." So I tried it out. And it did not work for me.

It didn't work for a number of reasons. One, like many of us, I was a creature of habit. The idea of doing something virtually that I had done in person for years did not come easily to me. For a long time, I'd been going to work and, during my lunch break, visiting the gym and meeting my trainer. With her, I'd do my circuit; she would hand me the weights and adjust the machines. When I stepped on the treadmill, she gave me goals to go faster and faster. This worked for me. And I liked the break in my day. I liked interacting with someone standing there, in person, doing the *Private Benjamin* thing or the Marines thing—encouraging me to go faster, jump higher. It was working for me. I felt no reason to change. The virtual experience left me wondering how that could be what I considered to be a workout. Training with someone on the phone? How would they pick out the right weights? It just seemed so out of the realm of reality. The fact that it was as much as 60 percent less in cost was irrelevant to me.

I did not see the virtual versus in-person training as an apple-for-apple exchange. I thought it was clever, absolutely. But it felt so far from the real experience. Fast forward to the early days of the pandemic, however—the gyms were all closed, and I was left to figure out how to work out in my den. My trainer called me and said, "Let's do a virtual session." She gave me a list of a few things to buy—a few bands, a few free weights—and used some creative approaches to craft my workouts. It turns out that you can, in fact, get a great workout with relatively few pieces of equipment. We made use of what I had (an ottoman in place of a box, for instance), pulled resistance bands, and did some squat thrusts. I trained with her weekly from my den and I . . . loved it. It was terrific. It was convenient. I still had the one-on-one time, and she was still able to yell at me—though now it was through my earbuds, telling me to go faster, work harder, sweat more.

When the gyms reopened, I didn't want to go back. The virtual had replaced the in-person.

A CLOSER LOOK: WONDERFULLY FUTURISTIC: THE EARLY DAYS OF PELOTON

While not a natural athlete, from his earliest days, keeping fit was always important to Peloton cofounder John Foley. The drive to stay fit and remain healthy never stopped as he reached adulthood. When he started dating Jill, who would become his wife, their dates revolved around fitness. After they had kids, they wanted to find ways to incorporate fitness into their daily routines. But finding fitness classes that would fit into their schedules, paying for fitness classes, and paying babysitters to watch the kids created obstacles to their desire to stay fit and healthy. It was also a matter of a tale as old as time: Jill remembered to book her spot in classes early and got spots in the classes she wanted with the instructors she liked. John, on the other hand, made his decisions to work out at the last minute and would often find himself locked out of what he wanted to do. John imagined that he wasn't the only one out there with what he calls "weak organizational skills," and this is what led him down the virtual path and brought him to the idea for Peloton.

This categorical disruption of the industry is not only changing the way people perceive and practice fitness, but it is putting a spotlight on businesses vying for consumer attention, both the existing and the emerging players. Among the newer players are those offering wearable fitness technology and guided workouts. Most notable among them is Apple Fitness+. Apple Fitness+ is designed to compete with not just platforms like Peloton but also real-world places, including the livestreams from your gym or personal trainers. It allows you to work out when and where you want, monitors your performance, and can keep track of your workout metrics using the sensor equipped on your Apple Watch.

More than the specifics of any virtual workout platform or method, and entirely aside from whatever issues Peloton has faced more recently, the lesson is this: disrupting the fitness industry is hard. It's very, very hard to get it exactly right. Yes, you heard me correctly. I am saying something that obvious because it needs to be said, remembered, and then remembered again regularly going forward.

When you look at something like Peloton, it's tempting to break it down into parts and fail to see the ingenuity of putting them all together in a discrete device. In this case, how is Peloton different than any stationary bike with an iPad playing a training video strapped to it? But if you look more closely, you will see how someone at Peloton took the time, effort, and attention to detail to create an entirely new version of the workout, one that would and could compete with the in-gym or otherwise in-person workout your body knows so well, offering a way to exercise with a trainer that is truly like having them in the room with you—and that this was a feat of engineering, in addition to one of ingenuity. Innovation like this all comes down to getting it right across all the various ways in which your customers experience your concept or product.

BRINGING YOGA INTO YOUR LIVING ROOM WITH A (NEARLY) HANDS-ON APPROACH

For years, the competition to dominate the world of fitness was about building better and more sophisticated gyms. Each one tried to outdo the other, adding new and increasingly sophisticated equipment, while accessorizing the experience with cooler juice bars and a select range of workout clothes in the shop. But these bells and whistles did little to make an argument for their superiority as havens for actual fitness. Bringing fitness into the digital realm, in many respects, meant starting the arms war all over again. Digital trainers, smartwatches, and apps that talk you through whatever your preferred exertion happens to be now abound. Even when a trainer is "live" on the screen, however, there has been an element missing that is now present in a yoga app called Yoganotch. The new frontier of fitness involves wearable technology, and it directs hyper-focused attention to how you move your body.

A large part of learning and gaining real mastery over a sport—be it tennis, skiing, or weight training—is having an expert or coach standing by to make sure your body is executing the moves correctly. This is rather important because, especially at the beginner level, we have limitless potential to hurt ourselves unwittingly.

"Drop your right hip and follow through, Allen."

"I am, I'm dropping it—and, wow, look at my follow through!" I respond.

This may sound familiar, especially the part where the trainer shakes their head and explains the many ways I, you, and most of us fail, at least initially, to execute what we've been instructed to do. In my mind, my form is always flawless and my body is responding perfectly to the many, many directives my ears hear and my brain directs it to do. The reality—what my trainer or coach sees—is almost always unrelated to what I see in my mind's eye. It's hard to be conscious of how your body is moving and to see with any accuracy what you are doing at any given moment. This is especially true of alignment that must be maintained with a body in motion.

This is what makes Yoganotch such an interesting proposition, especially during those times when our ability to meet in person can ebb and flow with little to no warning—though the ability to throw down a mat and "asana yourself" into good health and a calmer state of mind is appealing even when in-person is an option.

I had an interesting conversation with Yoganotch's founders, Eszter Ozsvald and Stepan Boltalin. Their yoga assistant allows you the flexibility of working out at home and combines it with the kind of attention and guidance you want from a yoga teacher. How? A smartphone app plus dime-size wearable sensors that allow the system to assess your form and offer guidance to make your practice safer and more effective. It's an extraordinary use of AI, one that allows an app to remind you to "square your hips" at the point when you actually need someone to say something about the position of your hips.

Yoganotch works for yogis of all levels, and the feedback is based on safety and maximum effectiveness. "Among the barriers to successful fitness," Ozsvald told me, "be it recreational sports like swimming or tennis or golf or yoga, is *how* you move. For yoga to be valuable, it's important to do the poses in the proper form, which also decreases the chance that you might be injured. The problem our technology solves is giving users better self-awareness of what they are doing, be it the right way or the wrong way."[4]

Yoganotch combines the best of yoga coaching with a creative use of cameras and sensors. It offers what it describes as "3D posture reconstruction" through the use of wearable sensors that analyze your posture in 3D space so that the app can then offer audio feedback to help correct your alignment. If you have done yoga even once, you will know the importance of alignment. It allows you to get the most out of your practice and to avoid rendering yourself a contorted, painful mess.

These wearable sensors are strategically placed on your legs, waist, and arms in order to offer a dynamic understanding of what is happening on your yoga mat. The feedback is available 24/7—and all this with the added bonus of feeling as if you've entered a sort of *Star Trek*-like Holodeck experience. Yoganotch has figured out a way to replicate the experience of having a trainer tell you that your arms are not parallel, that your hips are not aligned with your knees, and that you are not, in fact, maintaining toes pointed toward the sky. As is always the case, the more feedback you receive, especially of the kind that repeats itself as you repeat your misadventures, the more likely you are to achieve a safe and more effective workout. And the sensors accumulate the data in such a way that, for those who are motivated, one can even track their progress. Have you conquered your tendency to favor your left side? Has your right hip opened up now that you are attending to it according to the audio guidance the app has provided?

While I don't practice yoga (I struggle enough with Pilates), Ozsvald and Boltalin helped me see how this innovative technology could have amazing applications for a variety of fitness or athletic regimens. Its precise motion-analysis technology is already being used by thousands of researchers, developers, and athletes at the top universities as well as major-league teams. Yoganotch is the first of the company's consumer applications, but it opens up the possibility for more high-tech fitness products that go beyond simple video streaming as a way to help people access personalized instruction and move with peak efficiency. Rather than offering a one-way experience, the technology enables a two-way experience that confirms not only whether you are moving but also whether you are moving well, safely, and effectively.[5]

Yoganotch takes remote fitness to a level that improves the quality of your workout and the safety of your practice, and it offers complete and absolute flexibility as to when and where you do it. It is virtual without the compromises that typically come with the shift to virtual. The digital and physical worlds are brought together in a fascinating way that may have been inspired by an unavoidable need (see: the COVID-19 pandemic) but leaves behind an option that is useful and holds appeal to many in any circumstance.

A LOCAL TREASURE TAKES ITS SHOW TO A BROADER AUDIENCE: BUTTERFIELD MARKET

Just as Warby Parker looked to make the experience of buying eyeglasses easier and more fun; Peloton, home fitness more compelling; and Stitch Fix, the experience of dressing for success more convenient, the owners of Butterfield Market recognized that, beyond offering their specific products, it would be by changing up the experience of shopping at their uptown NYC location that they would differentiate themselves from competitors. What did this change involve? Interestingly, before the COVID-19 pandemic made outside dining and curbside pickup a requirement, Butterfield Market had the idea to install the equivalent of fast-food windows where people could order and pick up their breakfast treats and coffee, their noontime sandwiches, or their take-home dinners. I spent some time talking with Butterfield Market CMO Joelle Obsatz, who described this thinking. "We do a lot of observing; our managers make regular suggestions to us. We're very involved with the staff; we listen when they come to us and take seriously what they suggest we do. Because we aren't a huge company, we have the flexibility to try things, knowing they might not all work."[6]

By zooming out from the high-quality food itself, the owners of Butterfield Market saw the opportunity to make the totality of the store experience better. They took the experience that fast-food establishments have used for years and made it work in a tony, urban setting. That Butterfield took off over the last year is not surprising. That it continues to be a customer pleaser is also not surprising. The organization rolled things out incrementally: "We had our frozen-yogurt window, which was always very popular in our original location for years," said Obsatz.

The simple change in experience has made the Butterfield Market brand more convenient and more relevant to its city-sidewalk customers, and even more so during the COVID-19 pandemic when bringing the inside to the outside became a necessity. "We just thought it would be easy for people to grab and go to the park," Obsatz told me. "And we thought that'd be a good way to test the waters and see how many people are around when it seemed the city was empty but it was clear people were out there with needs. So we decided to offer sandwiches and salads—minimal [and] easy to package in a grab-and-go way—just to see if people would feel safer buying it that way. That's when we opened the window for the convenience of people to be able to shop in a different way."[7]

This frictionless and more expedient way to interact with the Butterfield Market brand is delighting its customers. The store's food products are still as wonderful as ever, but, as I've said, it's not just the products that make for success in today's market. With the decline of product differentiation as a means to competitive advantage, businesses and brands are increasingly looking at disrupting *experiences* as a way to differentiate their offerings.[8]

A CLOSER LOOK: TO LEARN, TO ANALYZE, ALL IN YOUR ZOOM WEAR: COURSEHORSE

While there is no shortage of options for people looking to increase their knowledge in a variety of skills and subjects, when Katie Kapler and Nihal Parthasarathi discovered that people were giving up on taking local classes because there was no organized method to search for them, they cofounded CourseHorse. When the pandemic hit their business, rather than pull back, they saw new opportunities to optimize their offering.

CourseHorse, which started as an aggregator of existing in-person class options and later segued into a vendor providing the virtual training itself, shows the extent to which the virtual option eliminates many of the barriers a traditional (live) path might have. In this case, the questions of where to physically hold a class and how a given location welcomes some attendees but leaves out others are entirely eliminated. From a purely logistical point of view, in a virtual setup, teachers are more available because they don't need to be in any particular place, classes aren't contingent on the availability of a physical space, and the timing of classes is more relaxed.

From there, determining what courses were not being offered, what information was not readily available, and then making them available with fewer logistical constraints enabled CourseHorse to fashion a product that felt bespoke without being individualized, something economical that allowed the experience to be largely dictated by the attendee who chose to join. In its original form, CourseHorse was an aggregator of courses in the universe, drawing from both the larger institutions and the incredibly small. They were made accessible on one platform, one registration space, one payment portal, with the ability to narrow choices by timing, price, availability, etc.

The experience—whether an individual seeking information, a group wanting to craft a particular experience, or a corporation in need of a team-building exercise—became the focus, one that was well within the grasp of these creative thinkers. At a certain point, the need to shift from marketplace to vendor was clear. Owning the product—instructor, platform, pricing—was the way forward in the fully virtual world.

Eventually, CourseHorse moved from classes that needed to appeal to a broad audience, which responded to an identified need and also introduced ideas that customers might not have thought of themselves, into the world of virtual team building. The pandemic made the reasoning behind this move obvious. Given the extent to which it seems that many industries will remain, at minimum, hybrid in their approach to personnel makes it clear that this is a tool that will be needed in the long run.

I spoke with David Golkin, former director of product strategy for CourseHorse, who described this pivot from marketplace to vendor: "It's less about a skill transfer because that's just much harder to do virtually . . . We want to define what is offered, how, and when. We learned really quickly [that] we want to own the full experience. And we want to own the relationships with instructors."[9]

"We developed courses that were effective, that brought people back to us again and again, no matter what the topic or need, [who] demanded we understand what it means to teach—teach well, effectively, enjoyably—in a virtual medium," Golkin told me.[10] He brought things down to what he knew about teaching first graders. Break things up into relatively small increments of time; mix up the means of messaging in those increments. After five to ten minutes of speaking, there needs to be a period of time to view slides, to ask the audience to engage with the material—something that shifts the brain from one mode to another.

The need for and value of virtual team building was not created by the pandemic. One of the challenges we had when I was at Landor, many years before the pandemic, was that we had four offices—in New York, Chicago, Cincinnati, and San Francisco. The offices had similar cultures, but there were always nuances to each office that reflected its history, when its team members joined, when we set it up, and the types of clients it worked with. It became clear that in order to reap the full benefits of all we were, we needed to assemble teams that pulled talent from multiple offices.

At various times, we pulled a strategy person from San Francisco, a creative from Cincinnati, and a research person from New York. It was then that the differences in culture and workstyle became clear. Old time budgets allowed for expensive gatherings to get the leadership teams together frequently enough to dull those edges, so there was coherence, at minimum, at the leadership level. Rarely, however, were whole offices and teams brought together, and our patchwork multi-city teams reflected the lack of integration. Physically gathering required the cost of moving many, many people around the country and coordinating a time to do so that would work for everyone.

CourseHorse's virtual training is not what many of us think of as traditional team building. Say this to most corporate workers, and images of group cooking classes or bowling tournaments will come to mind—big groups of people, with as much of the hierarchy removed as possible, experiencing one another as humans, not just as their professional roles. What CourseHorse offers is a dynamic way to replace but not replicate the spirit of such exercises while removing the cost (physical and monetary) to execute them in the physical world.

Golkin described the process of developing offerings that could compete with the real world whether or not the real world was available at any given moment. "When you think of online games, you picture cool, flashy graphics with a really smooth user experience," he said. "But that didn't address what companies want, which was a really engaged experience, where teammates were able to truly connect with each other. Amazing graphics, online games, only go so far. But if it doesn't allow me to connect with a teammate I haven't seen in person in a year, it's not achieving its goal."[11]

He continued,

How, then, do we take a real-life experience and transfer that to the virtual world? We thought, for a real-life pub trivia, all it takes is an emcee, a piece of paper, and an ability to talk only to those people on your team. And I thought, Zoom has that, right? You can use breakout rooms to mimic the little conversations that happen at a bar. We could easily recreate a new tool online that could do the answer-sheet part of it. And we needed to create, smooth, and perfect the process quickly. The initial forays were hacky and choppy. [But,] we quickly learned, people didn't mind. We saw that people

were coming back to us, even though we had a very unpolished fin-
ished experience in terms of the actual tool. What we were hitting
the mark on was the actual goal, which was interactiveness.[12]

CourseHorse went on to develop things like Lego events (mailing out
kits and tape measures for challenges like building the tallest tower) and
gingerbread-house making and, again and again, found that people wanted
what it had to offer. And what it offered came at a very reasonable cost.

Ultimately, Golkin learned, you should

always design for your grandmother. Always offer alternatives.
For trivia, for example, there will always be someone who doesn't
know how to open the window, who doesn't come into things
knowing what you expect them to know. You need to be able to
quickly say, "Hey, here's an alternative: grab a piece of paper and
hold onto these three things," right? You must make sure you have
a solution for the lowest common denominator in order to fully
address usability. Why? Because that person can derail an event. As
hosts, we learned this and had the control over the experience to
put measures in place to address them.[13]

---

*Virtual may feel like the most obvious lens right now. But it is—as it always
has been—the most challenging. You want to aim to create a meaningful
experience virtually, one that can stand up to comparison with and even
beat real-life options. This requires you to know what you are offering,
grasp the technology on which you rely to offer it, understand within an
inch precisely what your clients want from their experience, and offer
them an experience that exceeds that expectation.*

This demands that you set aside the idea of recreating the live experience and focus instead on creating a new experience entirely. What does that mean for your business? The truly effective virtual experience should improve upon reality, doing things we can't do in person. Leave behind our quotidian use of Zoom—a talking head, badly lit, with a PowerPoint deck clicking away—and think experientially about all that the virtual offers that the real world cannot. What are those ideas that would normally come and go, declared impossible to put into real life, constrained by the realities of physics or linear time? I know I sound as if I'm pitching a new sci-fi series, but what I'm really doing is asking you to look into your own ideas and see the virtual as opportunity to take the impossible and make it a virtual reality.

Lens 8

GETTING CLOSE TO THE CUSTOMER

Getting closer to the customer has always been the goal. The closer you are, the better the chance you have of conveying the worthiness of what you are offering. Simple. There are those who rely on others to sell or make the sale possible and those that hop over that step and create ways (online and in real time) to whisper (or shout) directly into the proverbial ears of their customers. This lens is about how you bring what you do literally closer to where the action is and do all you can to eliminate the need to rely on others to convey your vision, to speak to what is unique about what you do and how you do it. At the heart of this lens is asking how, within your industry or segment thereof, you can remove the need to rely on outlets and distributors to support, pitch, and sell what you do.

Certainly, getting close to the customer has long been Marketing 101. In my earlier days working with P&G, we would go to consumers' homes and watch them do everyday things like washing the dishes. We would watch them at the kitchen sink, noting, "Gee, isn't that interesting"—because, inevitably, what happened in the real world would be different than what the consumers themselves would describe when asked about these tasks during our qualitative research. Also in those days, Coke's mission was to be ubiquitous—its goal was to be within arm's reach when you were thirsty. Kodak was similarly poised, striving to be anywhere you were taking pictures.

There are a variety of approaches to this kind of proximity. Everyone believes they are customer-centric, and most will find a way to say as much in their pitch, on their website, and in any discussion of what they do and how they do it. What they don't realize, however, is the extent to which customer centricity is a concept most don't fully understand. As marketing professor Kevin Keller explained it to me, "Empathy is the most important thing. And you have to learn how to see through the eyes—you have to know how to walk in the shoes of your customers."[1] How you secure that level of knowledge varies, but if it isn't your explicit goal, your understanding of how you can transform customers' experience will always fall short.

At P&G, one of the world's largest manufacturers of consumer packaged goods, there's a well-known maxim about the critical importance of using "packaging to help tell the story and close the sale." When you know your customer well enough to know the color, shape, and form they will respond to (and buy), that is proximity. But that package has to be where a customer can see it. In this category, and so many others, one of the biggest barriers to success is getting closer to the customer.

MAKING YOUR PRODUCT DANCE ON THE SHELVES

Packaging has, historically, been about as close as you can get to a customer when you rely on others to actually put your product out in the world. It's your last chance, right at the moment when a customer's making a decision, to persuade consumers to buy. The effort put into packaging cannot be underestimated. It's what causes the hand that is reaching out to the options on the shelf to move closer or further away from where your product sits. Packaging is the last chance for you to tell your story about your product to the person you hope to make your customer. In the old days, this made the cost of placement for stand-alone displays, shelf talkers, and the like entirely worth whatever it was. The time available to you to tell your story, catch someone's eye, and make that sale was measured in seconds, and that is the job of packaging.

The early days of marketing set things up for this natural progression. When I was in marketing decades ago at Unilever, where it was called "product management," we spent most of our time trying to close the gap with the best tools we had at that time. We tried all sorts of ways to push the retailer to allow us to say to the consumer, "Hey, look at me" and "Hey, here's why I'm good" and "While I have you, here's a coupon while you're in the store to make buying our product just a little easier and a bit easier on the wallet, too." We had to do this dance because we were not there; we were not able to engage with the consumer directly. We had to hope that if we put our product in a store and that store received customers, they would find their way to us.

When I worked in the food industry—at what was then General Foods and which later became part of Kraft—we even did in-store sampling, setting up a table and encouraging people, one by one, to try us. But we couldn't be in every store and, bite for bite, it was not an economical approach to creating an audience. This was before social media, before a time when a bite could be captured for posterity in a picture, posted with exclamations of wonder and delight and shared with thousands of that person's closest and not-so-close friends. Today's world is a far cry from the one-at-a-time way of yore, which had logistical, economic, and practical challenges.

A CLOSER LOOK: AIRLINES LEARN TO TALK TO THEIR PASSENGERS: DELTA

Many years ago when I was working with Delta Airlines, we knew that one of the most significant customer-service challenges was when there was a flight change or delay or, worse, cancellation. With only one gate agent behind the counter and hundreds of frustrated fliers, with a voice among many echoing over the loudspeaker, we were doomed to be the bad guy in such a situation, no matter what we did. How could we improve this? Technology, of course, has now improved this scenario. But before the tech world stepped up its game, we made changes our competitors immediately replicated. We installed large-screen TVs at the gate, offering more information in view of more people. We set them up to offer information more generally to assuage what are the root causes of flier anger: confusion and lack of information.

We got close to the consumer by bringing the information they needed closer to them. We spoke directly to them despite the fact that, at the time, the screens were a significant investment. Delta took full advantage of the investment to speak directly with its fliers, to make it possible for fliers to go directly to whatever service they needed from Delta, and, in the end, to keep fliers close throughout the flying experience.

Quite literally, this is the path to reducing the space between you and those who buy what you make or sell. How do you take your message and put it in front of the eyes or in the hands of your customer? There are a number of traditional means to this particular end, including packaging and product placement in retail outlets. However, these rely on partners, the quality of which will vary. They are not always willing or able to do our bidding, and they are also limited by the sheer number of other partners taking up space on their shelves.

Why the haste to proximity? You want to take whatever it is you are offering—an isolated aspect of your business or the whole kit and caboodle—and remove the specter of the middle person to the greatest extent possible. Closing the distance means controlling the definition of your product to your consumer in as many senses as possible. Where once it was about placement in a supermarket (eye level to the average woman costs more than placement on lower shelves), now the moment of truth is in the unboxing on a table, preferably with the computer camera on, a YouTube, Instagram, or TikTok video in the making. The experience of unboxing, shared with communities for whom the unveiling means a shared experience that leads to identification with your brand and future sales, is just one of the experiences you can create in this proximate space.

A CLOSER LOOK: HOW APPLE BROUGHT THE CUSTOMERS TO THEM

In 2001 Apple was faced with a quandary. It had a product that was sold through traditional computer retail outlets. The problem: it was a tiny corner of the personal-computer market, and the vast majority of those who worked at traditional computer retail outlets knew nothing about Apple products. Apple needed to close the information gap between the design of its products and consumer understanding of what those products offered. At that point, 90 percent of the world was using PCs. It was as if the salesperson spoke a different language than the one required to sell an Apple product. They could not explain how Apple computers worked, much less why they were better and worth the higher price point. Mac was a new breed of computing device.

Apple was facing a tremendous obstacle with literally every aspect of the product it sought to disseminate. It didn't look familiar, its user interface was start-to-finish different from that of a PC, it was more expensive, and, before Apple Stores, there were few places to buy them. In electronics sales spaces, few people could advise on purchases and, once purchasers got products home, few support specialists were available to help teach users how to use them. For all intents and purposes, Apple was creating a new product category and needed millions of converts to be successful.

Buying a Mac required education and help from salespeople who understood the brand's magic and the technology. Apple understood that its job was twofold and quite distinct. Driving interest in its product was one thing. Creating an environment—and experience—in which potential buyers were guided by retailers who understood the products and who could explain what they did, how they did it, and why the premium pricing made sense was what Apple needed to control from start to finish. Big-box electronics stores had salespeople selling on commission. They didn't want employees spending too much time with one customer before moving on to the next. In addition, the typical electronics-store employee had no experience with Apple products, couldn't make an argument for spending more to shift platforms, and was unable to be of assistance post-sale.

Like with so many of the other aspects of its brand, Apple looked at an innovative way to solve a problem. It opened its own retail stores staffed by zealots whose enthusiasm about its product was real and true and tangible. They had both the knowledge and the passion to convey the *how* and *why* of the question "Why Apple?" Not only could they control the buying process and help bridge the information gap between its products and the consumer; they also disrupted how technological products were sold. They created an experience that starts when someone decides to "go Apple" and continues for the entire life of their involvement in the Apple universe. This includes support after your purchase—sessions on how to use a device when you are new to tech, repair services, guidance at the Genius Bar, approved and complementary ancillary products, and the launch and distribution of new product lines.

IT SHOULDN'T BE SO DIFFICULT TO PUT GLASSES ON YOUR FACE: WARBY PARKER

So many ideas start with a problem. In the case of Warby Parker, founders Neil Blumenthal, Andrew Hunt, David Gilboa, and Jeffrey Raider were students, one of whom lost his glasses on a backpacking trip. The cost of replacing them at a traditional optical retailer in Philadelphia was so high, he spent the first semester of graduate school without glasses, squinting and complaining.

And it wasn't just the cost. It was the old-school way retailers functioned. You, pointing at pairs of glasses that the salesperson did or did not correctly identify, a salesperson who often brought relatively little expertise to the process and who, in fact, slowed it down and made it difficult to make a choice about which you likely didn't care for their opinion. The news that you would then wait days, if not a week, for those glasses to come back with your prescription filled did not improve the experience.

The founders wondered where this experience might be streamlined to better reflect the needs and preferences of a new generation of frame consumers. A little research revealed that most of the glasses sold were sourced from just a few places, a phenomenal lack of competition that explained the extraordinarily high cost of the frames. Those manufacturers controlled the relationship with the retailers, and the retailers were bound by prices and options offered to them by these finite sources.

Warby Parker decided to get closer to its consumer. First, that meant being online-only, allowing people to choose frames in a new way. Then, it moved to brick-and-mortar shops that had an almost self-help quality to them. Then, it moved its salespeople out in front of the cases. You still picked up the frames yourself; you walked around and viewed yourself from the angles that meant the most to you. Just as Sephora put you in front of your makeup options and made it possible for you to try on products, Warby Parker gave you the glasses and the way to move through the choice process without dragging a salesperson along for the ride unless you wanted one. And if you did, that salesperson was friendly and limited their interaction (by training) to what was most helpful to you. If you wanted, you could go to the website, choose your lens, upload your prescription, and have your glasses sent to you. The retail outlets offered the same shipping options, saving that return trip.

It was fresh, and it was friendly. For a generation already hardwired to turn to the internet, the dual-platform options—bricks and mortar or online—simply made sense. Meeting the consumer where they live—in this case, both online and in a store that reflects their needs and price point—is the very definition of closing the distance. Warby Parker controls and defines everything about its brand and each thing it sells, and it offers services with a consistency that customers need to establish brand loyalty. Warby Parker took things one step further by creating an environment and process that reflected how its customers lived. You can ask for three frames to be sent to you at home, and then you can take pictures and post them and ask your friends on social media to help you make the decision. Today's consumers have no use for the traditional paradigm of the retail glasses shop and the person there whose opinion has no bearing on their life. Warby Parker changed the experience, and it disrupted the industry.

LUNCHES THAT FLY

Sometimes, getting closer to the customer is really about finding a new way to get closer to your customer. Dr. Samantha Sterling, chief strategy officer at design and innovation agency AKQA across Asia-Pacific, described an interesting solution being brought to a lunchtime challenge her company faces in China. You have a densely populated, tall office building in Shanghai and an entire building full of people who eat lunch at generally the same time. The simple act of getting out of the building to a place where lunch can be bought would take longer than the typical lunch break. Even sending enough delivery people into the building to serve the workers would preclude a timely arrival. The answer: drones. Local restaurants take online orders from the workers. Forty to fifty lunches are packed up at a time and sent out on small drones that land on the roof of the building. From there, they can be distributed downward efficiently and without creating a traffic jam.

This is, of course, making use of a cool, new-ish technology. Who doesn't think lunch is more fun when you know it arrived by drone? But for our purposes, it points to the need to examine a question or challenge from as many directions and perspectives as possible. Sometimes, this means literally. In this case, looking at the issue not from street level but from the sky allowed for a solution that brought the restaurants closer to those office workers they wished to serve.

A CLOSER LOOK: AMAZON KNOWS HOW OFTEN YOU BUY TOILET PAPER

Amazon has certainly redefined the way everyone buys and the expectations the customer has of the places from which they buy. This has been fueled by making the online-delivery path one that is controlled entirely by Amazon. Two-day, one-day, same-day, two-hour—these are the increments in which Amazon has taught us to think. Short of setting up shop on the curb outside your home or office building (and it might feel that way as their distribution centers proliferate further and further), Amazon has done everything it can to stand shoulder-to-shoulder with its customer. Its initial foray into bricks and mortar, seemingly the ultimate in getting close, failed because it seemed to take it further away. Choosing an extremely narrow range of options and placing the retail in areas that competed directly with those who had been there all along was an experiment that was declared over by the end of 2021.

Interestingly, as Amanda Mull discusses in her fascinating article "People Liked Malls" in the *Atlantic,* Amazon almost immediately unveiled plans for a new line of attack for sidling into proximity of its customer, a new take on an old idea: department stores. Thirty thousand square feet, carrying name brands as well as its own, Amazon would cover traditional content like clothes, electronics, and housewares. The point Mull makes is that, having revolutionized shopping by bringing so many to the point of digital exclusivity, Amazon's continued forays into real-time, real-place retail speaks to an understanding Mull frames like this: "Some things are just better done in person, both logistically and spiritually . . . no matter how much you streamline product search or payments processing, physical objects still exist in the world."[2] And, she points out, what goes out might (and often does) need to go back in the form of returns. Easy returns are the bedrock of removing friction, making it easier to come up close to your customer, though they cost everyone time and resources.

Getting close to the customer means getting through what the retail industry calls "the last mile." The move to digital meant everyone scrambled to manage quality control over how the thing you have gets to the person who wants it. Amazon is big enough to all but own its delivery channel and still struggles to meet the logistical demands that shipping entails at times. As Mull so elegantly points out, having killed the department store, Amazon stands primed (yes) to step in and fill the hole that was left. Furniture and other larger items are simply better sold in person (sit on it, and you will know) and definitely best sold with some finality (how do you print your own label to return a sofa?). Mull's conclusion makes sense: Amazon is defining what will stay in the digital universe and what needs, for any number of reasons, to be out in the world.

It's not a simple formulation for any business, even the giants. Jeremy Dawkins, global head of design at ?What If!, told me,

> We're looking at all the things which people at Walmart face as physical exclusions, and online just seems to answer all of them, you know, and yet what we're recognizing is it also compounds things like loneliness and isolation. The *Atlantic* piece by Amanda Mull suggests the fastest delivery method is going and picking it up. She's making the case that what Amazon needs to do is actually just have physical locations. But my Walmart client is saying, "Well, we've got the physical locations." What people want is some new experience, which is between [pickup] and traditional buying. Literally, don't wait online or in line. I think we're seeing quite strong indications that this may lead to a fairly radical new type of retail. What we're seeing is a bit of a shake-up of what shopping looks like. Is there another one which is an odd hybrid return to something very traditional?[3]

For the purposes of understanding how that math is done, you have to look at the various aspects of what you do and how it is sold, distributed, considered, and, yes, sometimes returned in order to know what "getting close to the customer" looks like for you.

A CLOSER LOOK: A NEIGHBORHOOD OR CITY'S INDEPENDENT BUSINESSES BROUGHT TO YOUR DOOR: DOORDASH AND INSTACART

The logistics and cost of running a website that accommodates ordering and maintaining a staff to pick up and deliver what you sell is simply beyond the capacity of the average small, independent business. Clunky, template-based websites turn off customers who expect a smooth, user-friendly interface. Adding to the responsibilities of your staff to coordinate pulling inventory or fare and preparing it to leave in a deliverable form can be insurmountable. Maintaining a delivery crew with no accurate sense of when or how much they will be needed is financially and practically speaking not feasible for most smaller entities.

And when fewer people started leaving their homes less and sticking closer to home when they did leave—yes, I'm talking about you, COVID-19 pandemic—these independent businesses were stuck betwixt and between. On the one hand, they didn't have the staff to burden with the additional tasks, and on the other, business was slow because their customers couldn't or wouldn't come to them, so they needed some way to get themselves to their customers. In other words, they needed a way to get closer to their customers who could no longer come to them.

Cooking Like His Mother

DoorDash cofounder Tony Xu is the son of a first-generation immigrant mother who worked in a restaurant. He knew firsthand how hard that business was, growing up watching his mom and washing dishes at the same place. He understood how vital these small restaurants are to the economy and the culture of a place. His passion was homegrown and inborn: How to help these independent restaurants get their food to more people? When he talks about the challenges faced when trying to set up a delivery system, he can picture it in his mind's eye. If you are most busy between 4 PM and 6 PM, what do you do with delivery people during the other hours? And even at the peak hour, affording enough delivery people to be able to offer the service reliably and quickly enough that customers might return is simply beyond the budget of so many businesses. Investing in a website, let alone one that could accept orders, was truly the stuff of fantasy. His passion was finding a way for local businesses to catch up.

Xu's journey started with a Stanford Business School project. He approached local restaurants and really drilled down into the nitty-gritty of what they could do and how their budgets worked. And he quizzed the local customers to find out what they wanted, needed, and wished were and were not the case. From the start, he understood there was something beyond the transactional aspects of what he was exploring; he wanted to understand the experience and understand it from everyone's perspective. He understood the importance of gathering that perspective before designing a solution.

Which brings us to the all-important element of any endeavor: the execution. Great ideas are, well, great. Not everyone has them. But the proof in the proverbial pudding is in the execution. People who can execute ideas well are incredibly rare. And it's what makes a business successful, especially an experience-centric business, because any one hiccup can ruin the overall experience, and then nothing else matters. Setting up a meal delivery is predicated on a setup that needs to work because all anyone will remember is that the cold food arrived an hour late. That'll be one customer who will not return. If they order off your platform, it's the platform that will take the hit. Consumers can forgive product snags here and there, but experience snags mean a human messed up, and they won't want to involve that human in their lives again. To succeed in the arena in which Xu set out, he really had to sweat the details.

At the start, he went out and experienced what it was like to do deliveries. What the ebb and flow of timing was like. How customers ordered off the website he built. What it took to plan for different times of day and days that signify different levels of need. Super Bowl Sunday was going to mean something to a pizza restaurant and to a wings-and-fries place, which required considering how to scale up so people wouldn't encounter wait times that would render the experience a negative one.

The details of setting up are one thing. He had to scale the project up and away from his initial pilot on the Stanford campus by hiring more drivers, making sure the right number of drivers were available at the right times, figuring out parking—all of the details. If you don't get into the minutiae, you're not going to solve the problem. A big part of Xu's strength was the drive to solve a problem that spoke to a personal quest combined with the business skill to build an organization that could execute at the level he did—because experience is hard to manage. It's about people: what and how they do things, how and why they respond to the way things are done. Humans are fallible, and the more people involved, the more difficult execution becomes.

As Stanford lecturer Robert Siegel puts it in a summary of a guest lecture Xu gave, "DoorDash is thus attempting to establish its basis of competitive advantage as they designed a solution from the beginning that addresses all of the parties in the three-sided market, and by understanding the needs of merchants in particular (who are currently not a part of a ride-sharing solution), DoorDash has a head start that becomes difficult for others to replicate if other systems were not designed for a three-sided market from day one."[4]

A CLOSER LOOK: THE GRIND OF GROCERY SHOPPING: INSTACART

In the case of Instacart founder Apoorva Mehta, he was a first-generation immigrant from Canada. In looking for a business idea, he had already been a part of one startup that, after the initial funding came in, he realized he simply wasn't passionate about. Mehta knew how hard it is to do a startup well, and he knew the only way it works is if you want to throw everything you have into it. It was a lesson learned.

Mehta then saw the challenges many grocery stores were having in keeping up with the general movement toward online ordering and delivery—specifically, in challenging Amazon for a place at its table. He pored over apps from all the big guys. He realized it wouldn't be too difficult to gather the data to put the inventory online. From a customer point of view, the problem in need of solving was that grocery shopping is really not fun. It feels like a particularly bad use of time, as Envirosell founder Paco Underhill pointed out to me. A vast majority of the items most customers buy at the supermarket is repetitive. If most of what you buy this week is what you bought last week, and you go to this grocery store because it has the things you buy over and over, why, oh why, are you schlepping to that store over and over? Instacart intended to bring the market—big and small—closer to the customer, so close that the customer needn't actually go there.

And then there are the details. Those pesky, experience-making, business make-or-break details. In the case of Instacart, it was the dilemma of what you do when your customer has ordered the 32-ounce Hellmann's mayonnaise but, when the shopper gets to the shelf, there are 12-ounce and 48-ounce but no 32-ounce bottles. Mehta thought to build into an app the ability for the shopper to reach out to the customer (by call or text) to see if they wanted the substitution. This was an act of getting closer to the customer to get them what they want rather than simply saying the store was out of what they'd specifically requested. Customers could feel the proximity, the human element rather than a bot or AI making a decision, which brought them, again, closer.

The initial goal was to offer a range of grocery-market options and make the shopping experience one that was reliable and that included communication. By offering not just the obvious contenders but also the specialty shops, the lesser-known markets, Mehta accomplished a number of things. He expanded those stores' ability to get close to customers they would otherwise not reach. People like supporting their local businesses. And he created a platform and approach that would appeal to the younger demographic: local, authentic, with a user interface that puts the action on their phones.

In 2012, Mehta launched Instacart. He became the first customer and shopper of his service, ordering groceries on his own grocery-delivery app and then picking them up and delivering them to himself.[5] He was the only one there, so it was going to have to be him. But he knew he had something other people would want to use if he could craft an experience that worked for enough customers and enough markets. Eventually, his friends started using the app, and then, after quite a bit of sharing, people he didn't know were stepping up and having an experience of his app that proved the solidity of his idea and execution.

A CLOSER LOOK: IT'S ALWAYS ABOUT THE EXECUTION: DOORDASH

At the heart of both DoorDash and Instacart is the impulse to take an eclectic, diverse, and variable group of businesses and bring them—en masse—closer to their customers (and even to create customers who may not know of them) by providing an online mechanism for ordering and delivering their wares. Both companies get these businesses closer to their customers by literally bringing what they do to their doorsteps.

The technology powering each was nothing new and was applicable to a range of offerings. For every small restaurant with a menu that never exceeds two dozen dishes, there is an independent supermarket with literally a thousand discrete items to choose from. In the end, though, both used basic technology that was readily available, even if it was beyond the budget of a given small business.

Both started with a website they were able to create and design quickly. The sophistication of the idea was in the experience it offered. This experience-driven idea was centered around the notion that people would benefit from—would *want*—the wide range of options that existed in their community. There are so many restaurants you might order from, but the smallest among them might not have their own delivery service for logistical reasons. There were people out there who needed to try the terrific Malaysian place or the Ethiopian one on the other side of the street—if only those places delivered. And some smaller grocery stores had more to offer than the generic grocery store that had the infrastructure to deliver and maintain a robust virtual interface.

This is not, of course, a straightforward tale of bringing customers closer to businesses. There is significant brokering at work here, as you can imagine: the business, the customers, and, in between, the shopping/driving/delivery fleet. And there were and are distinct challenges to each element at play. Who takes the financial hit when there is a problem with an order? How do you orchestrate the billing at all? The list is endless. But the impetus for each had to do with bringing businesses and customers closer together.

A CLOSER LOOK: WHO BROUGHT US TOGETHER WHEN WE HAD TO BE APART? ZOOM

Zoom didn't always trip off the lips with the ease it does now. Always a solid option in the video-conferencing world, there were and are other perfectly viable options: Microsoft Teams, WebEx, GoToMeeting among them. The reason Zoom won out when the world went remote was simple: it was simple. No software to download. Nothing to learn to do. You don't even have to have passwords. It's a link, a URL, just like sharing anything online is. You could send it to even the most tech-phobic and inept person you know and say, "Click on that, and I will appear on the screen," and your meeting would still happen.

In other words, Zoom made it possible for us to easily "get close" to one another, including our customers. Because we used it at work and at home, and because we were often in the same spaces while using it, Zoom entered the fabric of all the various parts of our lives. This, to the tune of 300 million daily meeting participants and 3.5 trillion annual meeting minutes.[6]

There are those that attribute its success, at least in part, to its name. Zoom has, as University of Nevada, Las Vegas, marketing professor Anjala S. Krishen points out, become the Band-Aid of pandemic life. As she explains, "Zoom employs sound symbolism . . . which is when a word describes a sound by imitating the actual sound." She elaborates,

> The name "Zoom" is also successful because it quite simply begins with the letter "z," which is a fricative: a consonant sound that blocks the passage of air moving through the mouth, generating audible friction. Brand names containing fricatives are perceived as smaller, faster, lighter, sharper, and softer. A 2014 study by business researchers Richard R. Klink and Lan Wu notes that the letter communicates efficacy.[7]

Zoom founder Eric Yuan attributes his longtime involvement in the world of telephony and videoconferencing to the long train ride he needed to take to visit his girlfriend while he was in school and both were still in China. His first startup was in college, where he developed a piece of bespoke video-telephony software.[8]

Yuan's story is well known and often told. He started at WebEx in 1997 as one of its founding engineers and rose to run a successful engineering team there. He left in 2011 with forty engineers after he failed to pitch a mobile-friendly video system. He started Zoom (originally called "Saasbee") the same year. The first-iteration beta was released in 2012, and Zoom 1.0 was available in January 2013. Zoom hit one million users in January 2013. Fast-forward to March 2020: Zoom was downloaded 2.13 million times in a single day.[9]

Yuan practices what he preaches. As he described in a 2019 *Forbes* article, he hired hundreds of people to work as engineers for Zoom in China and then went three years without visiting the office in which they worked. He approached fundraising in a similarly remote manner, showing up only once to a pitch, and only to make sure everyone had downloaded the app. He treated remote meetings as the only way to meet well before this was an established concept. The article mentions that he left his headquarters in San Jose for exactly one investor lunch in San Francisco, heading back to San Jose the same day. Everyone else, big investor or small, met with him on Zoom. At one point, he'd made only eight work trips in five years.[10] The point is that this is technology that has long allowed people who may be physically distant to join and truly communicate with clients and customers.

"Customers have always said, 'Eric, we'll become your very important customer, you've got to visit us,'" says Yuan. "I say, 'Fine, I'm going to visit you, but let's have a Zoom call first.' That's usually enough."[11] It's that "enough" that makes this a story of bringing people closer together. For many, they didn't know how well, deeply, and importantly they could communicate with a customer or client virtually until that became their only option. And they learned what Yuan knew and dedicated his working life to developing.

It is enough, even preferred, but only if it works, is easy to use, and makes it possible to communicate with a broad swath of people. And when teleconferencing was first developed, none of that was the case. Clumsy equipment, unstable connections, terrible sound and video, and, worse, requiring everyone to be on the same platform, with the same thing downloaded and understanding how the mechanics worked—none of that is easy. None of that will ever be enough. Zoom is a simple and direct way to access to your customers.

Getting close to the customer is about more than proximity. It's about an intimacy of knowledge and a grasp of nuance. There is an emotional benefit to getting close in this way because when a consumer is closer to you, their experience will feel more personal, richer, and, well, better.

I'm reminded of an old British Airways commercial[12] that I've always loved, which spoke to the role it saw itself playing in the lives of its customers. In the commercial, we meet first a twenty-something Ratnesh, who tells us he is from what he still thinks of as Bombay, India. Then we meet his mother, Alka, who describes her trepidation and sadness when the time came for her son to move far away. She goes on to say that she has been given a seat on a British Airways flight, which will fly her home-cooked food to her son. She tells us, "I think this will make him come home and visit his mummy." She knows that even without being told, once he tastes her food, he will know from whom it came. The final scene is one in which Ratnesh, his mother, and his father are gathered together in a loving reunion. His mother shares with us that she is disciplining herself not to ask him when he will be leaving: "I will not ask you today. Let this question be for tomorrow."

British Airways has positioned itself as the airline that brings families together, which offers the opportunity for communication and transport to come together into one, heartstring-pulling moment.

To offer an experience that is granular, that responds to what consumers haven't even considered, is the key to getting close and doing what others cannot do. It's understanding what is in people's hearts, what their wishes are, and what will make the human experience richer, more meaningful.

In Conclusion

I hope this book will serve as a guiding light for your journey to transforming the stuff we do and reimagining your company or brand through experience. These lenses provide different ways to look at the marketplace. They help you spot opportunities to change the way we do things that others typically miss or don't see clearly. These different perspectives provide a clarity that allows you to see the opportunities that exist in the world.

To use these lenses optimally, you need to prime your eyes to see what others have yet to notice. It's best to use fresh eyes, eyes that defy the traditional training we all receive when we enter the business world. Bring a little of the old-fashioned, Jerry Seinfeld–esque "Have you ever noticed . . . ?" to the situation and be willing to point to and talk about the obvious, the thing staring us in the face that no one sees.

Diversity matters. One set of eyes on a situation or idea or problem will very rarely net the results of a group of eyes all looking from different places, ages, experiences, and expertise. If everyone has the same hard-wiring, everyone will look at the world the same way no matter what lenses they look through, and opportunities will be missed. I do not joke when I say: pretend to be an alien from another planet, and then describe your day. Question everything. Dissect every act, every intention, every assumption. Just for a moment, avoid bringing the rivers of knowledge that make you as smart, as creative, as successful as you've always been. Let yourself be the one who has to have it all explained to them.

Seeing opportunities is interesting, but it's not a direct line to success. Many are the products or companies that started with a great observation of a need or new way of doing something. But only a few can connect seeing something to seizing the opportunity. The most important characteristic of an opportunity seized successfully? A brilliant execution. And that is among the hardest things in the world to do.

To execute at this level, you will need time to figure out how to deliver on the promise, how to iterate, how to improve, and how to learn from mistakes. The way to create the time to do it right is to be the first one with the idea. Let's face it; while it's still early in the transition from internal combustion engines to electric mobility, it's clear even at this stage that the head start Tesla had by seeing the opportunity and the need for the transition ahead of all the traditional carmakers gave it years alone in the industry to iterate and develop and execute on how to use electric cars to solve our mobility challenges, to work out what kind of battery power is needed, the best software to extend the battery life, and the right type of components to speed up the charging process. Tesla worked on all of this (and more) while all the other car companies were optimizing the internal combustion engine and getting better performance and smoother acceleration. Now that the industry as a whole is dipping its collective toes into the electric-car pool, the rest are just playing catch-up. The work they all did in the recent past with the combustible engines was not necessarily time well spent.

The electric-car conundrum is one that is far more complicated than what I've just described, but it does speak to where resources spent on anticipatory and predictive projects can be well worth your while. The most important thing about the lenses I've provided to you is that they can give you a head start, and they can give you a few extra moments to figure out and perfect how you'll execute your idea—and that is what you need to succeed in the marketplace.

All of which is to say that before you begin your journey, follow some of my suggestions to get you to the starting line. I see myself as a way of cleaning your glasses, if you will. The process of getting your head in the game and looking clearly at what is happening in the marketplace today is one that requires a clarity of vision and an ear that is attuned for nuance. When you walk in your customers' shoes, you can be empathetic to their lives and their challenges in a way that will make it possible to transform the experiences that make up their lives. Only then will you be able to get inside their heads and understand what they are really thinking, feeling, fearing, and wanting.

EXPERTS AREN'T ALWAYS THE ANSWER; SOMETIMES, THEY'RE PART OF THE PROBLEM

Getting ready to look means being able to open your eyes and truly see what is in front of you. This is what the Buddhists call a "beginner's mind."

In the business world, when you go to a company, you will meet lots of people who have all been in the business for years. This is one of their claims to fame, in fact. Pharma, diapers, soap, beer—teams work together and remain in the same industry for years and know it inside and out. But it is highly unlikely that such people are seeing anything with new eyes or a beginner's mind. No one on such a team is questioning, "Why have we always done it that way?" There are a lot of ideas and methods that are on autopilot. The common refrain is "This is how we do things; this is how we've always done things."

Don't get me wrong—there is a benefit and value of experts. We don't want them all to leave the room. But risk enters when everyone gets used to doing things a certain way and stops seeing what is happening in front of them. It's sort of like the wallpaper in your kitchen. Someone comes in and comments, "That wallpaper looks really dated. Do you know how long that has been up?" And you look at it and say, "It looks fine to me." And then, of course, you can't help but look at it with fresh eyes and say, "Actually, you know, you're right. This is really out of style." Fresh eyes, clear vision, and so on.

So, in addition to a diverse team, the other dimension you need is to recruit people from outside your category who can look at it and question its assumptions. Opportunities are incredibly hard to see. To see them takes effort; it takes hearing things that may make you, as one in the category, uncomfortable.

When your scope is narrow and your voices are few, you are more inclined to hear only from the so-called experts. The more focused their expertise, it would seem, the better. For instance, if someone is an expert in beer, specifically beer that is made and bottled in the western region of the United States, you have someone who knows a lot about a very narrow range of information. If you are in the beer industry, this person will bring some information to the table, but they are also unlikely to offer much in the way of how one might break out of sales patterns and packaging that has been used thus far.

Dr. Samantha Sterling of AKQA, where she is the chief strategy officer across Asia-Pacific, takes this idea very much to heart. She pointed out to me that the companies who focus on hiring employees with years of experience in a certain category have certain benefits. There is less risk and less training involved in bringing them on board. But, as she explained to me, "It limits a firm's ability to see opportunities. We're a little different. We try to prevent people who are customers of a category from working in that category. So, if you are really into running, we avoid [having you work] on a running brand.

"This can be hard because people obviously want to work on the thing that they're excited about. And the client wants that person because they think it gives them shortcuts, but it doesn't help with this kind of work . . . Some of the best strategists I've worked with have been biologists and chemists and aeronautical engineers because the way they view the world brings something to the table that everyone else doesn't notice anymore, if ever."[1]

Genuine curiosity that is unburdened by preconceived notions and history—this is where innovation that leads to a change of customer behavior is born.

THE ART OF SEEING WHAT IS INVISIBLE TO OTHERS

Jonathan Swift, satirist and author of, most famously, *Gulliver's Travels*, would have made a great marketer. He was a great observer of the human condition, and his best-known book is, in essence, about the art of seeing what is invisible to others. It is about having vision.

The best marketers have vision. Vision comes from insights about things others don't see. Customer insight is key for any business endeavor. Consumer insights are an interpretation of human behavior that aims to uncover the underlying preferences, frustrations, and motivations of a consumer so that your offering—whatever it is—can respond to something they need or a question they would have asked, if only they'd thought to do so. By understanding how consumers think and feel, you can build a deeper empathy that understands not just what they need but why they need it.

Few things in marketing, however, are more challenging than understanding a consumer's wants, needs, or desires. And in a marketplace that is increasingly transformed by the forces of globalization, technology, and social and cultural revolutions, not to mention the world events of 2020 and beyond, this has become even more challenging. If you think all you have to do is ask a consumer what they want, think again.

BRING ON THE NEW

Award-winning film and television producer Brian Grazer says he's always had an insatiable curiosity. He set the goal of meeting a new person every day. "I turned it into a discipline. It was a religion to me," he says. "I could not feel fulfilled unless I met that new person every day."

This is how he met his close friend and longtime business partner Ron Howard. It was 1979, and Grazer was inside his office on the lot of Paramount Pictures wondering to whom he would talk that day. "I thought, God, I have to meet a new person today. I haven't checked someone off the list," he says. "I look out my window—I'm on the Paramount lot—and I see Ron Howard, who was *Happy Days*'s Richie."

That Grazer is among the most prolific in the entertainment industry is obvious. How he came to be so is not just because he is talented, which he is, but also because he is curious. In fact, he has been called "the most curious man in Hollywood." Grazer has spent most of his life indulging that curiosity through what he terms "curiosity conversations" with some of the most interesting people in the world, including spies, royals, scientists, politicians, athletes, moguls, Nobel laureates, artists, and anybody he believes has a story that will broaden his worldview. Some of these conversations led to many of his movies and TV shows.

Each of our eight lenses offers a different perspective, and each one allows you to see opportunity from different vantage points. I'd like to say that if you just immerse yourself in this book's thinking and truly bring it to bear on your industry or project or problem, you'll be set to go. I wish it were that easy.

My first job was at Ogilvy & Mather, and it was an extraordinarily wonderful place for training. It hired lots of young people right out of college or business school, and it held a formal training program once a week during which you learned the basics of how to create powerful advertising from the firm's amazing leaders. The company even went so far as to create a series of guides, which it called "Magic Lanterns," that offered powerful principles and ways to make advertising more effective, taken from the wisdom of David Ogilvy and the experience of the agency and its leaders.

The Magic Lantern takeaway? Have the pictures, tell the story, show the product working, use humor to focus on the benefit and not the problem, keep it simple . . . the list goes on and on. And I can confirm from firsthand experience that using these guiding principles often helps you develop more effective advertising. It really does.

But it is also true that the best ideas came from the creative teams that broke all the rules. And while it is true that, having broken all the rules initially, the follow-through that provided the focus and the sharpening often meant a return to Magic Lantern principles, it started with something outside of the box. Principles are terrific and useful and need to be learned. But principles are only helpful for increasing your chances that your answer will be effective—they don't give you the answer itself.

The principles that formed the core of Ogilvy's Magic Lanterns have to be used judiciously because they are a support system, not the idea generator. Principles are good theories to help you think better and increase your odds of success, and they will definitely help you see things that others might not. Principles are the discipline behind the creative process. But one of the things I've learned throughout my career is that what separates success and failure is seeing the idea ahead of the pack—seeing it first, seeing down the road and around the corner. This is accomplished by bringing together a diversified team of creative and nonlinear thinkers and starting with fresh eyes. With that kind of team, the execution has to be brilliant. What drives the marketplace is execution. The iPad wasn't the first tablet on the market; HP had one, Microsoft had one, Dell had one. But Apple got the execution spot on. It nailed the user interface, designed the product, made it work out of the box without twenty pages of instructions, made it so simple that a literal three-year-old could pronounce its name and make it work, packaged it exquisitely, and then presented it not as a tool to be used behind someone's desk but as something someone could use sitting on a sofa with it on their knee. Apple got it right from concept to execution. Getting it right doesn't mean 80 percent right, and it doesn't mean 85 percent right. The ones that win come in around 99 percent right. That's where the sweat comes in. That's where the grit comes in.

GET OUT OF YOUR COMFORT ZONE

For many years, I did not have a client in the consumer-electronics space. As I mentioned, that did not stop me from going to the annual Consumer Electronics Show, where thousands of companies from across the globe come together to showcase the latest in digital health, food tech, automotive tech, NFTs, gaming, smart homes, and much more. It's geek nirvana, for sure, but it's also an incredible place to see what's happening in the world outside your own industry, not to mention that there's just a lot of awe-inspiring stuff.

Get out into the world and go where you have no business being. If you're in tech, go to a food-and-wine conference; if you're in food and wine, go to a toy or gift fair. No matter what field or endeavor you're working on, go to Comic-Con and get ideas from people who love comic books, science fiction, and fantasy literature. If you keep doing the same old thing, you'll keep seeing the same old results and keep thinking the same old ways.

Be on the lookout for intersections between behavioral, technological, and demographic trends. For example, mobile communications, social networking, a comfort with ephemera, and the short attention spans of millennials led to the creation of Tinder, a GPS-linked matchmaker.

If you're in IT and only talk to others in IT, that is the only perspective you'll get. Bring people onto your team who are from a variety of disciplines. A number of major corporations have used this tactic from the very top down to give their organizations a push in a new, more competitive direction.

On this note, I was deeply saddened to hear of the death of Brian Goldner, former CEO of Hasbro. He oversaw a company whose brands include My Little Pony, Monopoly, Dungeons & Dragons, Power Rangers, and Nerf. Coming to the company in 2008, Goldner had worked at the J. Walter Thompson advertising agency, where he rose to the director in charge of entertainment before leaving to join Bandai America, a subsidiary of a Japanese toy company. Seeing the possibilities outside the normal parameters of the category, he turned Hasbro, a traditional maker of toys and games, into an entertainment company with its own TV and movie studio.

One of his most significant successes was persuading Hollywood executives that Hasbro toys and action figures like Transformers and G.I. Joe were as film worthy as Batman or Spider-Man. "We had relegated these brands to an experience that was limited to the playroom floor or kitchen table," Goldner told the *New York Times* in 2009.[2] What he envisioned for the company was something more expansive. Taking a page from Theodore Levitt's playbook, Goldner saw the opportunities inherent in defining the toy industry more broadly, and Hasbro was perceptive enough to add him to its team.

The way to take the broadest view and gain the greatest perspective involves thinking that comes from a range of people, perspectives, and expertise. Bringing a cross-disciplined group of people to a discussion produces ideas that allow the unseen to be seen, the quiet murmur to be heard. When P&G did this with ten people from ten different disciplines at one table, Claudia Kotchka, the former P&G vice president of design innovation and strategy, told me, "What we heard from all the people on those teams was 'This is the first time I was able to bring my whole self to the job.' We [had] put people in buckets: 'If you're in finance, stick with those numbers of yours.' When you let them loose with each other, this is diverse thinking. You've got cognitive diversity on a team because they see different things, they hear different things. And that is magic."[3]

Figuring out how to bring that magic to what you do, to your thinking—this is what we are here to do.

Acknowledgments

A few words of gratitude.

I would not be the man I am today—son, father, husband, and marketing professional—were it not for my father. Like other suburban dads, Joe Adamson taught my brother and me how to ride a bike, throw a baseball, play tennis, and drive a car. He showed us the right way to wash the car, wear a tie, and cut the grass. Growing up, other than his accent, I discerned very little difference between my dad and my friends' dads. That came later.

Born Ernst Joachim Adamsohn in Konigsberg, Germany, on June 4, 1924, my dad had to move in with his grandparents in Berlin at the age of four after his father died of a heart attack and the family went bankrupt. Soon, everything changed even more dramatically as Hitler's hold on power grew stronger through the 1930s. My dad was taunted and beaten up by boys in brown Hitler Youth uniforms. Then, on November 9, 1938 (Kristallnacht), his grandfather was killed while neighbors ransacked their home.

A few days later, my dad's mother took him to a train station and sent him off, with only a small suitcase in hand, via train and boat on the "children's transport" to Southampton, England. Upon arrival, two nuns met him and brought him to Westgate-on-the-Sea, across the English Channel from Belgium. He arrived alone, not speaking a word of English, and began school. After finishing school, my dad moved to London during the height of the Blitz. Taking shelter from German bombs was a regular part of his life. More than this, he worked as an air-raid warden, spending nights in the London Underground.

During the worst part of the war in London, my dad was lucky enough to be recruited by the American Army as an intelligence officer, joining the US Air Force 32nd Bomb Squadron. He traveled across Europe with

the troops, interrogating German prisoners of war and joining forces with those liberating the Mauthausen Concentration Camp.

After the war, my dad arrived in New York City on the *Queen Elizabeth*—again with only a small suitcase in hand—ready and able to realize the American Dream.

It wasn't until I was older that I began to learn the details of my dad's incredible journey. He didn't talk about his expulsion from his home, his lonely life in England, and, most critically, his exposure to the atrocities of World War II and the Holocaust. What my dad witnessed and experienced shaped his view of life and became the lens through which he approached life—and taught him lessons on how to live life fully, meaningfully, and joyfully. Joe Adamson taught me these lessons without speaking them aloud. Be resilient, have grit, and have faith in your built-in navigation system to redirect when facing obstacles. These lessons continue to shape my worldview. As my dad told an interviewer shortly before his death, "Many people came out of that environment and collapsed completely. You only live once and must make the most of it. Yes, whatever happened is terrible, but you can't make it your way of life."

Acknowledgments

Though Joe Adamson was born into a privileged family in Germany with a seemingly comfortable and easy path forward, that path was destroyed. He was left on his own to figure things out and learn to be self-sufficient in every sense of the word. He had no family to fall back on for help, no backstop or safety net. But rather than making him bitter, his experience made him stronger, more sensitive, and more eager to embrace life.

The sense of resilience I picked up from my dad has been like rocket fuel. It has allowed me to meet challenges and face adversity head-on. It has taught me to look forward, not backward, and power through disappointments and bumps in the road. Most importantly, it has enabled me to see and feel gratitude for what I have.

He was always optimistic. His business had good and bad times, but he always maintained an upbeat attitude. Despite everything he endured, during all the traumas of his youth, he would visualize happier times and move forward. He found meaning and purpose day to day and truly seized every day he lived.

My dad always made time for us, having dinner every night with his family. My memories of childhood include everything from putting up tents in the backyard to the annual setting up of Lionel trains, each year with new layouts and interesting new railway cars. His focus on family has been a source of strength for me throughout my life. It has been my experience that a strong family is like a launchpad for life, pointing you in the right direction, giving you the drive to get you where you want to go. My dad gave me a Saturn V launchpad.

Dad, I think of you and miss you every day.

As with all my previous books, this one again required the partnership and support of many to go from "This might make an interesting book" to being able to hit "Send" on my Mac.

Acknowledgments

The first thank-you goes to my longtime book partner Betsy Karp. Betsy worked with me for over a year to refine and crystallize the core premise and foundation necessary to capture several publishers' interest.

Second, to my editing partner, Elizabeth Bogner, who had to engage in endless Vulcan mind melds with me to extract clarity, focus, and structure from a sea of thoughts floating in my head.

Next to my assistant, Elisa Roland, who survived the two-year journey managing more than sixty interviews, researching context, fact-checking, and looking over countless drafts.

Most importantly, thank you to my wife, Madelyn, and my children, Elissa and Josh, for their support and encouragement. The answer is clear when friends ask me what motivates me to write another book. Many years ago, my children, then fifteen and eleven, wandered into a bookstore on a family vacation to Oxford, England. In the business section, they found one of my books and insisted on having a picture taken of them holding it. That picture floating by on my screen saver every few days always brings a smile to my face—and, sometimes, a tear to my eye.

And a final thank-you to Zoe, our family dog for almost sixteen years, for bringing joy to our home every day. She was all about our children for the first part of her life. Once the kids grew up, Zoe became my shadow and was by my side every hour for the three years I worked on this book until her last day.

Notes

Introduction

1. Claudia Kotchka (former vice president of design innovation and strategy, P&G), in discussion with the author, January 5, 2022.

See the How: Get Ready for Experience Innovation

1. Douglas Martin (chief brand and disruptive-growth officer, General Mills), in discussion with the author, February 24, 2022.
2. Kevin Lane Keller, Brain Sternthal, and Alice M. Tybout, "Three Questions You Need to Ask About Your Brand," *Harvard Business Review*, September 2002, https://hbr.org/2002/09/three-questions-you-need-to-ask-about-your-brand.
3. Claudia Kotchka, in discussion with the author, January 5, 2022.
4. Leslie Zane (founder and CEO, Triggers® Brand Consulting), in discussion with the author, December 29, 2021.
5. Rajeev Batra (Sebastian S. Kresge Professor of Marketing, Ross School of Business, University of Michigan), in discussion with the author, September 3, 2022.
6. Leslie Zane, in discussion with the author, December 29, 2021.
7. Leslie Zane, in discussion with the author, December 29, 2021.
8. Jeremy Dawkins (global head of design, ?What If!), in discussion with the author, September 1, 2021.
9. Antonio Belloni (group managing director, LVMH), in discussion with the author, January 13, 2022.
10. Antonio Belloni, in discussion with the author, January 13, 2022.

Lens 1: Focus In & Drill Down

1. Bill Heilman (media partner, Metaforce), in discussion with the author, January 24, 2022.
2. Bill Heilman, in discussion with the author, January 24, 2022.

3   Steven Fuld (senior vice president of marketing, Sony), in discussion with the author, September 1, 2021.

4   Steven Fuld, in discussion with the author, September 1, 2021.

5   Guy Raz, "Calendly: Tope Awotona," September 14, 2020, in *How I Built This*, produced by NPR, podcast, 1:14:14, https://www.npr.org/2020/09/11/911960189/calendly-tope-awotona.

6   Tope Awotona, "Calendly: Tope Awotona," September 14, 2020, in *How I Built This*, produced by NPR, podcast, 1:14:14, https://www.npr.org/2020/09/11/911960189/calendly-tope-awotona.

7   Kevin Keller (E. B. Osborn Professor of Marketing, Tuck School of Business, Dartmouth College), in discussion with the author, March 3, 2022.

8   Kevin Keller, in discussion with the author, March 3, 2022.

9   Guy Raz, in discussion with the author, September 2, 2021.

10   Guy Raz, in discussion with the author, September 2, 2021.

11   Guy Raz, in discussion with the author, September 2, 2021.

12   Jack Caporal, "Gen Z and Millennial Investors: Ranking the Most Used, Trusted Investing Tools," *The Motley Fool*, August 3, 2021, https://www.fool.com/research/gen-z-millennial -investors-tools/.

13   Caporal, "Gen Z and Millennial Investors."

14   Marcel Schwantes, "Steve Jobs's Advice on the Only 4 Times You Should Say No Is Brilliant," *Inc.*, January 31, 2018, https://www.inc.com/marcel-schwantes/first-90-days-steve-jobs-advice -on-the-only-4-times-you-should-say-no.html.

Lens 2: Customize and Make It Personal

1   Bob Pittman (cofounder, MTV; chairman and CEO, iHeartMedia), in discussion with the author, March 29, 2022.

2   Bob Pittman, in discussion with the author, March 29, 2022.

3   Erik Lindecrantz, Madeleine Tjon Pian Gi, and Stefano Zerbi, "Personalizing the Customer Experience: Driving Differentiation in Retail," *McKinsey & Company*, April 28, 2020, https://www .mckinsey.com/industries/retail/our-insights/personalizing-the-customer-experience-driving -differentiation-in-retail.

4   Paco Underhill (founder, Envirosell), in discussion with the author, August 2, 2021.

5   Erik Lindecrantz, Madeleine Tjon Pian Gi, and Stefano Zerbi, "Personalizing the Customer Experience: Driving Differentiation in Retail."

6   Katie Ryan (group planning director, BBDO), in discussion with the author, September 10, 2021.

7   Oded Koenigsberg (professor of marketing, London Business School), in discussion with the author, November 30, 2021.

8   Oded Koenigsberg, in discussion with the author, November 30 2021.

9   Allen Adamson and Joel Steckel, *Shift Ahead: How the Best Companies Stay Relevant in a Fast- Changing World* (New York: AMACOM, 2017).

10   Gary Briggs (former CMO, Facebook), in discussion with the author, March 1, 2022.

11   Gary Briggs, in discussion with the author, March 1, 2022.

12   Gary Briggs, in discussion with the author, March 1, 2022.

13   Mary Ann Azevedo, "WeWork Unbundles Its Products in an Attempt to Make Itself Over, but Will the Strategy Work?", *TechCrunch*, March 15, 2021, https://techcrunch.com/2021/03/15/ wework-unbundles-its-products-in-an-attempt-to-make-itself-over-but-will-the-strategy-work/.

14   Mary Ann Azevedo, "WeWork Unbundles Its Products in an Attempt to Make Itself Over, but Will the Strategy Work?"

15   Dr. Samantha Sterling (chief strategy officer, APAC, AKQA), in discussion with the author, October 19, 2021.

16   Aaron Brooks, "30 Killer Examples of Personalised Customer Experiences," Venture Harbour, February 7, 2022, https://www.ventureharbour.com/personalised-experiences-examples/.

17   Katrina Lake, "Stitch Fix's CEO on Selling Personal Style to the Mass Market," *Harvard Business Review*, May–June 2018, https://hbr.org/2018/05/stitch-fixs-ceo-on-selling-personal-style-to-the-mass-market.

Lens 3: Joining Forces

1   Allen Adamson and Joel Steckel, *Shift Ahead: How the Best Companies Stay Relevant in a Fast-Changing World* (New York: AMACOM, 2017).

2   Guy Raz, "Casper: Philip Krim," June 28, 2021, in *How I Built This*, produced by NPR, podcast, 1:22:53, https://www.npr.org/2021/06/23/1009551702/casper-philip-krim.

3   Richard Feloni, "Audible's founder talks about selling his company to Amazon for $300 million, bonding with Jeff Bezos, and how he managed to have a 'nontoxic' midlife crisis (AMZN)," *Yahoo! News*, April 22, 2018, https://www.yahoo.com/news/audible-apos-founder-talks-selling-182422149.htmlg.

4   Mitch Ratcliffe (partner and sustainability marketing practice lead, Metaforce), in discussion with the author, January 29, 2022.

5   Mitch Ratcliffe, in discussion with the author, January 29, 2022.

6   Guy Raz, "Audible: Don Katz," November 1, 2021, in *How I Built This*, produced by NPR, podcast, 1:17:22, https://www.npr.org/2021/10/29/1050511655/audible-don-katz.

7   Guy Raz, in discussion with the author, September 2, 2021.

8   Guy Raz, "Audible: Don Katz."

9   Mitch Ratcliffe, in discussion with the author, January 29, 2022.

10   Guy Raz, in discussion with the author, September 2, 2021.

11   Guy Raz, in discussion with the author, September 2, 2021.

12   Guy Raz, "Audible: Don Katz."

13   Allen Adamson and Joel Steckel, *Shift Ahead: How the Best Companies Stay Relevant in a Fast-Changing World*.

14   Allen Adamson and Joel Steckel, *Shift Ahead: How the Best Companies Stay Relevant in a Fast-Changing World*.

15   Noah Brodsky (chief commercial officer, Lindblad Expeditions), in discussion with the author, August 9, 2022.

Lens 4: See Like a Concierge

1   Stephanie Resendes, "The Hospitality Quotient: Danny Meyer's Hiring Formula for Building a Brand," Upserve, February 6, 2020, https://upserve.com/restaurant-insider/the-hospitality-quotient/.

2   Stephanie Resendes, "The Hospitality Quotient: Danny Meyer's Hiring Formula for Building a Brand."

3   Cassie Holmes (professor, UCLA Anderson School of Management), in discussion with the author, September 9, 2021.

4   Cassie Holmes, in discussion with the author, September 9, 2021.

5   Chip Bell, "Are You Delivering Concierge Customer Service?" *Forbes*, October 1, 2020, https://www.forbes.com/sites/chipbell/2020/10/01/are-you-delivering-concierge-customer-service/?sh=3adf6558704f.

6   Bob Pittman, in discussion with the author, March 29, 2022.

7   Suzy Deering (former global CMO, Ford), in discussion with the author, March 30, 2022.

8   Suzy Deering, in discussion with the author, March 30, 2022.

9   Suzy Deering, in discussion with the author, March 30, 2022.

10   Suzy Deering, in discussion with the author, March 30, 2022.

11   Suzy Deering, in discussion with the author, March 30, 2022.

12   Sodexo homepage, accessed September 20, 2022, https://us.sodexo.com/home.html.

13   Ronni Schorr (global vice president of marketing, Circles Concierge), in discussion with the author, April 25, 2022.

14   Ronni Schorr, in discussion with the author, April 25, 2022.

15   Ronni Schorr, in discussion with the author, April 25, 2022.

16   Ronni Schorr, in discussion with the author, April 25, 2022.

17   "Popular Jerry Seinfeld Quotes," TVFANATIC, accessed September 20, 2022, https://www.tvfanatic.com/quotes/characters/jerry-seinfeld/by-views/page-7.html.

Lens 5: Go the Rental Route

1   Dan Winston (former VP of market operations, Spin), in discussion with the author, March 22, 2022.

2   Jennifer Hyman, "A Letter from Our Co-Founder and CEO Jennifer Y. Hyman," Rent the Runway Investor Relations Page, accessed September 20, 2022, https://investors.renttherunway.com/founders-letter.

3   Jamie Friedlander, "How Jennifer Hyman Is Disrupting the Way We Get Dressed," *Success*, November 13, 2017, https://www.success.com/how-jennifer-hyman-is-disrupting-the-way-we-get-dressed/.

4   Jackelyn Ho, "What Do You Do When Someone Doesn't Want to Meet with You? Rent the Runway's Co-Founder Says to Show Up Anyway," *Inc*, https://www.inc.com/jackelyn-ho/what-do-you-do-when-someone-doesnt-want-to-meet-wi.html.

5   Heather Wood Rudulph, "How Jennifer Hyman Completely Changed the Way Women Shop," *Cosmopolitan*, April 28, 2016, https://www.cosmopolitan.com/career/a57537/jennifer-hyman-rent-the-runway/

6   "Rent The Runway: Jenn Hyman," August 6, 2017, in *How I Built This*, produced by NPR, podcast, 54:00:00, https://www.npr.org/2017/09/21/541686055/rent-the-runway-jenn-hyman.

7   "Jennifer Hyman, "Jennifer Hyman: Rethinking Rental in a Crisis," The Business of Fashion, February 25, 2021, YouTube video, 17:05, https://youtu.be/l6QoMdcS1DA.

8   "Rent The Runway: Jenn Hyman," in *How I Built This*.

9   Oded Koenigsberg, in discussion with the author, November 30, 2021.

10 Marco Bertini and Oded Koenigsberg, *The Ends Game: How Smart Companies Stop Selling Products and Start Delivering Value* (Cambridge, MA: The MIT Press, 2020).

11 Tony Leopold (senior vice president of strategy, digital, and business development, United Rentals), in discussion with the author, April 22, 2022.

12 Tony Leopold, in discussion with the author, April 22, 2022.

13 Tony Leopold, in discussion with the author, April 22, 2022.

14 *Seinfeld*, season 3, episode 11, directed by Tom Cherones, aired December 4, 1991, on NBC.

Lens 6: Approach Things as a Broker

1   "Online Dating Is Booming, Changing in Pandemic Era," Arizona State University Office of the University Provost, February 8, 2022, https://provost.asu.edu/online-dating-booming-changing-pandemic-era.

2   Dr. Samantha Sterling, in discussion with the author, October 19, 2021.

3   James Casio, "Mad Men. The Definitive List of All 27 Pitches." *Deadicated Fans*, December 5, 2020, https://deadicatedfans.com/poll/mad-men-the-definitive-list-of-all-27-pitches-pick-your-favorite/

4   Guy Raz, in discussion with the author, September 2, 2021.

5   Zhi Hao Liu, "3 Easy Ways to Personalize Your Guest Experience," TurnoverBnB, December 7, 2021, https://turnoverbnb.com/3-easy-ways-to-personalize-your-guest-experience/.

6   *Groundhog Day*, directed by Harold Ramis (Columbia Pictures, 1993).

7   "Policygenius: Jennifer Fitzgerald," May 24, 2021, in *How I Built This*, produced by NPR, podcast, 1:20:32, https://www.npr.org/2021/05/21/999062490/policygenius-jennifer-fitzgerald.

8   "Policygenius: Jennifer Fitzgerald," in *How I Built This*.

9   "Policygenius: Jennifer Fitzgerald," in *How I Built This*.

10   "Policygenius: Jennifer Fitzgerald," in *How I Built This*.

11   "Policygenius: Jennifer Fitzgerald," in *How I Built This*.

12   Christine Hall, "WoodSpoon's Food Delivery Service Cooks up Support for Home Chefs with $14M Round," *TechCrunch*, August 10, 2021, https://techcrunch.com/2021/08/10/woodspoons-food-delivery-service-cooks-up-support-for-home-chefs-with-14m-round/.

Lens 7: Explore Virtual Options

1   Bob Smith (director of classroom innovation, Stanford University), in discussion with the author, August 27, 2021.

2   Summer Moore Batte, "The Zoom Where It Happens," *Stanford Magazine*, May 2021, https://stanfordmag.org/contents/the-zoom-where-it-happens.

3   Bob Smith, in discussion with the author, August 28, 2021.

4   Allen Adamson, "Apple Fitness+ Is Just the Start of the Next Wave to Disrupt the Fitness Industry," *Forbes*, February 14, 2021, https://www.forbes.com/sites/allenadamson/2021/02/14/apple-fitness--is-just-the-start-of-the-next-wave-to-disrupt-the-fitness-industry/?sh=68bce3713143.

5   Allen Adamson, "Apple Fitness+ Is Just the Start of the Next Wave to Disrupt the Fitness Industry."

6   Joelle Obsatz (CMO, Butterfield Market), in discussion with the author, June 18, 2022.

7   Joelle Obsatz, in discussion with the author, June 18, 2022.

8   Allen Adamson, "It's Disruptive Experiences, Not Products, That Drive Success in Today's Market," *Forbes*, July 8, 2021, https://www.forbes.com/sites/allenadamson/2021/07/08/its-disruptive-experiences-not-products-that-drive-success-in-todays-market/?sh=68d1eebd7913.

9   David Golkin (former director of product strategy, CourseHorse), in discussion with the author, January 30, 2022.

10   David Golkin, in discussion with the author, January 30, 2022.

11   David Golkin, in discussion with the author, January 30, 2022.

12   David Golkin, in discussion with the author, January 30, 2022.

13   David Golkin, in discussion with the author, January 30, 2022.

Lens 8: Getting Close to the Customer

1   Kevin Keller, in discussion with the author, August 3, 2021.

2   Amanda Mull, "People Liked Malls," *Atlantic*, August 21, 2021, https://www.theatlantic.com/technology/archive/2021/08/amazon-department-stores-prime-shipping/619860/.

3   Jeremy Dawkins, in discussion with the author, September 1, 2021.

4   Robert Siegel, "The Complexity of Marketplaces—Tony Xu, CEO DoorDash," *Medium*, March 9, 2017, https://medium.com/the-industrialist-s-dilemma/the-complexity-of-marketplaces-tony-xu-ceo-doordash-61441cd25269.

5   "How Instacart Founder Apoorva Mehta Became a Billionaire," *Sugermint*, accessed September 26, 2022, https://sugermint.com/apoorva-mehta-instacart-founder/.

6   Dominic Kent, "The History of Eric Yuan's Zoom," https://dispatch.m.io.erie-yuan-zoom/.

7   Anjala S. Krishen, "How 'Zoom' became the 'Kleenex' of Video Calling," *Fast Company*, May 24, 2021, https://www.fastcompany.com/90639158/zoom-naming-strategy.

8   Kent, "The History of Eric Yuan's Zoom."

9   Kent, "The History of Eric Yuan's Zoom."

10   Alex Konrad, "Zoom, Zoom, Zoom! The Exclusive Inside Story of the New Billionaire Behind Tech's Hottest IPO," *Forbes,* April 19, 2019, https://www.forbes.com/sites/alexkonrad/2019/04/19/zoom-zoom-zoom-the-exclusive-inside-story-of-the-new-billionaire-behind-techs-hottest-ipo/?sh=14f608884af1.

11   Alex Konrad, "Zoom, Zoom, Zoom!"

12   British Airways, "British Airways India – A Ticket to Visit Mum," July 29, 2013, YouTube video, 5:20, https://youtu.be/WPcfJuk1t8s.

In Conclusion

1   Dr. Samantha Sterling, in discussion with the author, October 19, 2021.

2   Dave Itzkoff, "The Movie Industry's New Playthings," *New York Times,* June 18, 2009, https://www.nytimes.com/2009/06/21/movies/21itzk.html.

3   Claudia Kotchka, in discussion with the author, January 5, 2022.

About the Author

For more than thirty years Allen Adamson has helped launch, nurture, and reinvent brands, ranging from startups, to nonprofits, to companies known worldwide, in categories including packaged goods, technology, health care, financial services, hospitality, and entertainment. His philosophy, substantiated time and again, is that successful brands stand for something that is both different and relevant—and simple for consumers to understand.

A noted industry expert in all disciplines of branding, Allen has worked on the agency side for several iconic firms, and on the client side for Unilever. He was chairman of Landor Associates, a global brand consultancy where, under his leadership, the company partnered with brands including Accenture, GE, Johnson & Johnson, FedEx, HBO, Marriott, MetLife, P&G, Sony, and Verizon. Additionally, he guided organizations including the 9/11 Memorial and Museum, the Central Park Conservancy, and the Council on Foreign Relations.

In addition to this book, Allen has shared his industry expertise in four previous books: *BrandSimple: How the Best Brands Keep it Simple and Succeed*; *BrandDigital: Simple Ways Top Brands Succeed in the Digital World*; *The Edge: 50 Tips from Brands that Lead*; and *Shift Ahead: How the Best Companies Stay Relevant in a Fast-Changing World*. He has also written a column on branding for *Forbes* for twenty years.

Allen is cofounder and managing partner of Metaforce (www.metaforce .com), a disruptive consultancy and activation firm which takes a multidisciplinary approach to marketing challenges. He is an adjunct professor at The Berkley Center for Entrepreneurship at NYU Stern School of Business.

Allen received his BS from the S.I. Newhouse School of Public Communications at Syracuse University and an MBA from New York University's Stern School of Business. Allen lives in New York City with his wife, Madelyn. Their two children, Josh and Elissa, do their best to help their father keep up with what's relevant.